GRAHAM GREENE: An Introduction to His Writings

NEW SERIES VOLUME XXXVIII

# COSTERUS

Amsterdam 1983

# GRAHAM GREENE:
# AN INTRODUCTION TO HIS WRITINGS

by

Henry J. Donaghy

Printed in the Netherlands
ISBN: 90-6203-535-3

To Joyce, Nora and Martin

CONTENTS

## CHRONOLOGY

1904: *Graham Greene is born on October 2 in Berkhamsted, Hertfordshire.*

*1920: He is sent for six months to stay with a psychiatrist, Kenneth Richmond, near Kensington Gardens.*

*1922-1925: Greene attends Balliol College, Oxford.*

*1923: To counteract boredom, he plays Russian roulette.*

*1925: Babbling April*, a book of verse, is published.

1926: Greene works for the Nottingham *Journal* and later, as sub-editor, for the *Times*. He becomes a Catholic.

1927: Marries Vivien Dayrell-Browning.

1929: *The Man Within*, Greene's first novel, is published.

1932: *Stamboul Train* is published and is first of Greene's novels made into a film. American title: *Orient Express.*

1934-1945: Greene walks across the heart of Liberia and discovers a love of life.

1934: *It's a Battlefield* is published.

1935: *The Basement Room*, a collection of stories, is published. Also *England Made Me*. In U.S.A. later reissued as *The Shipwreck-ed.*

1936: *Journey Without Maps*, based on the African journey, is published. Also *A Gun For Sale*. American title: *This Gun For Hire*.

1937-1938: He journeys to Mexico to report on religious persecution there, does so in *The Lawless Roads* (1939).

1938: *Brighton Rock* is published.

1939: *The Confidential Agent* is published.

1940: *The Power and Glory* is published. American title: *The Labyrinthine Ways*.

1942: *British Dramatists*, a historical survey of drama in England, is published.

1942-1943: Greene works for the British Secret Intelligence Service in Sierra Leone, Africa.

1943: *The Ministry of Fear* is published.

1947: *Nineteen Stories* is published.

1948: *The Heart of the Matter* is published. *The Fallen Idol*, one of Greene's most successful films, appears. It is taken from his story, The Basement Room. He visits Czechoslovakia and Vienna.

1949: *The Third Man*, one of Greene's most successful films, appears. A year later the novel is published.

1951: *The End of the Affair* and *The Lost Childhood and Other Essays* are published. Greene travels to Malaya and to Indo-China for the first time.

1953: *The Living Room*, Greene's first drama, is published. Also *Essais Catholiques*, six essays translated from English.

1954: *Twenty-One Stories* is published.

1955: *Loser Takes All* and *The Quiet American* are published.

1957: *The Potting Shed*, a drama, is published. He goes to Cuba a second time, also to China and to Russia.

1958: Greene becomes a director of the Bodley Head publishing house. *Our Man in Havana* is published.

1959: *The Complaisant Lover*, a drama, is published.

1961: *A Burnt-Out Case* and *In Search of A Character*, journals of two African trips, are published.

1963: *A Sense of Reality*, a collection of stories, is published.

1964: *Carving A Statue*, his fourth drama, is published. He travels to Santo Domingo.

1966: *The Comedians* is published.

1967: *May We Borrow Your Husband*, a collection of stories, is published. He travels to Israel and to Dahomey, where *The Comedians* is filmed.

1969: *Collected Essays* and *Travels With My Aunt* are published. He travels to Paraguay and Argentina.

1971: *A Sort of Life*, an autobiography covering Greene's life until about 1930 is published.

1973: *The Honorary Consul* is published.

1974: *Lord Rochester's Monkey*, a biography essential written years before, is published.

1975: *The Return of A.J. Raffles,* a drama is published.

1978: *The Human Factor* is published.

1980: *Doctor Fischer of Geneva or the Bomb Party* is published.

# Preface

Far from turning to new interests after completing his last "theological" novel, *The End of the Affair* (1951), Graham Greene has been consistent and unrelenting in his themes over the course of the past 50 years. These themes are more fundamental than the religious problems of his middle period. They include such concerns as the divided self, the betrayal of a friend, justifiable suicide, and the real presence of supernatural evil in the world. Such dominant concerns are seen as early as *The Man Within* (1929) and perdure through the present. Moreover, Greene's perspective as a writer has always been the one he described in his "virtue of disloyalty" address at the University of Hamburg: "The writer is driven by his own vocation to be a protestant in a Catholic society, a catholic in a Protestant one, to see the virtues of a capitalist in a Communist society, of the communist in a Capitalist state. . . . He stands for the victims, and the victims change. Loyalty confines you to accepted opinions. Loyalty forbids you to comprehend sympathetically your dissident fellow; but disloyalty encourages you to roam through any human mind; it gives the novelist an extra dimension of understanding." Though this book is not primarily intended to argue a thesis but rather to introduce the common reader to the novels of Greene, to the peculiar strengths and weaknesses of each novel, the novelist's enduring themes and perspective are kept steadily before the reader's eyes.

To help the reader see the genesis of Greene's ideas, the first chapter discusses the major events of and influences upon Greene's life. The facts of that life will make evident where Greene's "obsessions" (to use his own word) come from. The obsession with betrayal, for example, will be seen as dating from a public-school trauma and the preoccupation with suicide probably belongs to the same school days, as well as to his love for a governess. The conviction that supernatural evil abounds in the world dates to early nightmares and to the reading of *Vipers of Milan* at fourteen years of age, though his understanding the reasons for that conviction did not come until he visited Liberia.

Nonetheless all these themes antedate Greene's religious conversion and his later concern with theological matters. Moreover, the reader will notice that other themes, like the need for engagement or the virtue of disloyalty, begin with Greene's first novel and continue to the present.

Thus, while certain themes receive greater or lesser emphasis at different stages in his career, Greene's concerns have been consistent. Religion helped him explain these concerns, and continues to do so, but it did not give rise to them.

I would like to thank H. Wayne Schow for reading this manuscript and for his constructive suggestions; I would also like to thank Rita Matthiesen for her typing and editorial help.

## Chapter One

## *LIFE AND INFLUENCE*

In his essay, "Henry James: The Private Universe," Graham Greene remarks: "It was just because the visible universe which he was so careful to treat with the highest kind of justice was determined for him at an early age that his family background is of such interest." For the same reason Greene's own family background is of interest.

Graham Greene was born on October 2, 1904 in the town of Berkhamsted, twenty-eight miles northwest of London. The fourth of six children, Graham was not especially close to his father, Charles Henry Greene. This might have been due to his father's position as headmaster of Berkhamsted School, which Graham himself attended. Nonetheless, the author tells us that he did not discover his father's love for him until he himself had children. School was a painful time. As son of the headmaster, he was not fully accepted by his peers, and he was not skillful enough at sports to partly redeem himself. Some of the boys took a sadistic delight in playing upon his ambiguous position. Two in particular, Carter and Watson, Greene never forgot. Carter was a real adept at turning the screw and Watson, the less vicious, had been a friend before going over to Carter. When in later years Greene met Watson in West Africa, he was astonished to learn Watson thought of their school-boy relationship as a close and friendly one. Perhaps Watson could not be expected to have understood the acute sensitivity of the young artist. Nonetheless, from the school-boy problems spring two very important results in Greene: his perduring theme of betrayal and, more importantly, the drive to excel as a writer. He tells us in his autobiography, *A Sort of Life*: "I wondered all the way back to my hotel if I would ever have written a book had it not been for Watson and the dead Carter, if those years of humiliation had not given me an excessive desire to prove that I was good at something, however long the effort might prove."

To these years belong Greene's first "suicide attempts." On different occasions he entered his mother's darkroom and drank hypo he thought poisonous, drained a bottle of hay fever pills, ate deadly nightshade, and once took twenty aspirin before swimming in the empty school pool. Though each instance had its effect, none succeeded in killing him.

Greene in fact has acknowledged that a "successful suicide is often only a cry for help which hasn't been heard in time."

In 1920, Greene's brother Raymond, then a medical student and later a successful physician, suggested that his father allow Graham to undergo psychoanalysis. The boy had complained of the filth at school and his father mistakenly supposed him the victim of a masturbation ring. At any rate, his father surprised young Graham by consenting to Raymond's suggestion. Graham, who may have been near to a nervous breakdown, was sent to live for six months with his analyst, Kenneth Richmond. This time in London, at Lancaster Gate on the north side of Kensington Gardens, Greene calls perhaps the happiest six months of his life. Away from the scatology of his school mates and the ambiguity of his own position at school, he breakfasted in bed, and met at Richmond's house his then favorite poet, Walter de la Mare. Kenneth Richmond seems to have done his job well because Greene returned a new boy. Of course it helped no longer to have to be a boarder at school, but he had also put behind him his hatred of classes and the domination of Carter and Watson.

Greene's flirtations with suicide, however, were not entirely over. Three years later, when he was 18, he fell in love with a woman, about 11 years older, who was employed as a governess for the younger Greene children, Hugh and Elizabeth. When this innocent, though very serious, love affair came to an end, Greene played Russian roulette for the first of several times. However, he insists this was not an attempt at suicide but a gamble calculated to relieve the boredom he now felt.

Though he repeated the gamble on other occasions, its effect wore off and he put this cure for boredom aside. Greene admitted recently to V. S. Pritchett that the bullets in the chamber might have been harmless or they would not have been left lying around.[1] Nevertheless, he seemed on the first try or so to believe them harmful enough or his reaction would not have been what it was. Still Greene is certainly right in seeing his play with the revolver as a gamble rather than suicide. When later, at the time of his marriage, he learned he was probably epileptic (a doctor's opinion apparently controverted by time), he tried to commit suicide by throwing himself from a London Underground platform in front of an oncoming train. He could not do it. There was no gamble there and no antidote for boredom.

While at Balliol College, Oxford, Greene sought a new relief for boredom and lost love. For virtually a whole semester he was drunk, going to bed at night intoxicated and resuming his drinking next morning. Fortunately, he became bored with that cure too. He turned for a short time to Communism, but mostly because he thought it would provide him a trip to Russia. When his motives were seen through, he ceased to attend meetings. The young intriguer also dallied, at Oxford, with German espionage when he offered his services to help the Germans protect the Palatinate from its French occupiers, who wished to appropriate it.

Finally, while still an undergraduate, Greene met the girl he was to marry. He had written a film review in which he referred to Catholics' "worship" of the Virgin Mary. Vivien Dayrell-Browning sent a note to him at Balliol, pointing out his error and distinguishing between "worship" and "hyperdulia," a form of reverence greater than that given to other saints but clearly not worship, which was reserved for God. Greene found interesting anyone who would take seriously such "subtle distinctions of an unbelievable theology" so he sought Miss Dayrell-Browning out. When he was keeping company with Vivien in 1925, he thought he owed it to her to learn more about her religion. Thus Greene dropped a note in the question box of the Cathedral in Nottingham, where he had come to work for the *Journal* since the London *Times* would not hire an inexperienced apprentice. And at Nottingham his instructions began.

Young Greene came to look forward to these instructions from Father Trollope, a man who had given up the stage he loved to enter the priesthood. Upon becoming a priest, Father Trollope could not even in those days attend the theatre. The two men would have the lessons in some odd places because Greene did not like to have weekly appointments cancelled, and Father Trollope had a busy and unpredictable schedule. Thus, their chats on Josephus or the authenticity of the Gospels might be held on the upper deck of a Nottingham bus.

Though it had not been Greene's intention to convert, merely to learn, he became a Catholic in February 1926. He was not at the time overwhelmed with faith. St. Thomas' five arguments for God's existence did not speak to him, as they did not to Father Trollope, but he could finally believe in some supreme being. He took the name Thomas, not after the Angelic Doctor, but after the Doubter. In his ambiguity here as in his ambiguity over his situation in his father's school, we might find the source of his persistent theme of the divided self.

Greene married, and he and Vivien had two children, a boy and a girl. He separated from his family a few years after the marriage but has been as scrupulous about guarding the privacy of his wife and children as he has been open and honest in speaking about himself.

Perhaps Greene offers a hint of the reason for his separation in the description of his paternal grandfather, William. In *A Sort of Life*, he tells us he identifies most closely with this man he calls a manic depressive — a description he has applied elsewhere to himself. William had gone to St. Kitts in the West Indies as a boy of sixteen and returned when he contracted yellow fever. Still, though not the need of money, something called him back to the West Indies. So this man, who could not involve himself in ordinary pursuits like his more successful brothers and who sensed a barrier between himself and his eight children, left wife and children and returned to St. Kitts in middle age. His family regretted his going but could not bring itself to follow his romantic example. To what extent the life of this grandfather to whom Greene feels closest offers a gloss upon the life of the author it may be tactless to speculate further, since the author has chosen to protect the privacy of his wife and children.

In January of 1926, Greene left the Nottingham *Journal* from which he had received no salary and began as sub-editor for the London *Times*. While retaining a great deal of affection for the *Journal* and for Nottingham, he learned the writer's craft at the *Times*. There he spent his time in the company of thoroughly experienced writers, there he learned to prune the cliches of reporters and to condense their stories without loss of meaning or effect, and he had his mornings free to do his own writing.

In the winter of 1928, as Greene lay in bed with the flu, Heinemann called to say that they had accepted *The Man Within* for publication. Now, too rashly, Greene decided to quit the *Times* and to make his living as a writer. When *The Name of Action* (1930) and *Rumour at Nightfall* (1931) proved disasters, Greene regretted his lack of a job. By 1932 his publishers, particularly his American publisher, Doubleday, were imposing very stringent financial arrangements upon him. After a successful, if callow, first novel, what had gone wrong with these next two works? Greene tells us he had tried to omit the autobiographical entirely and, as a result, the novels lacked life and truth, seemed like warmed-over Conrad. Greene had to learn a difficult lesson in the use of autobiography, as we will see at the conclusion of this chapter.

In 1934 Greene took the first of a seemingly endless series of trips to other parts of the world. With his cousin Barbara, he walked without maps across the heart of Liberia. Recorded in his *Journey Without Maps* (1936), the trip was surely rash for someone who knew nothing of Africa, but it also proved one of the turning points of his life. Though one who had always thought death desirable, Greene discovered in himself a passionate love of living. He even came, if not to love the rats in the huts where he slept, to accept them calmly as a part of life. "I was discovering in myself a thing I thought I had never possessed: a love of life."

Greene also discovered in Liberia the archetypal basis for his earliest nightmares. The frightening creatures of those dreams were not in the beginning evil things trying to come in but devils in the African sense of beings who control power. However, mankind has corrupted these primitive realities, has denied its inherited sense of supernatural evil, and reduced it to the level of human evil. "It isn't a gain to have turned the witch or the masked secret dancer, the sense of supernatural evil, into the small human viciousness of the thin distinguished military grey head in Kensington Gardens with the soft lips and the eye which dwelt with dull lustre on girls and boys of a certain age." To so corrupt is to forget "the finer taste, the finer pleasure, the finer terror on which we might have built." Greene then had found the human basis for themes that persistently made their way into his novels.

Though the hardships endured on his African trek were great, they were not so bad as those endured a couple of years later when in 1937 Greene visited Mexico. He had been asked to report on religious persecution in the country, and he chose its most primitive provinces, Tabasco and Chiapas. Travelling through these states via boat, burro, bus, and, in two mountainous parts, airplane, Greene never came to love the country as he had Liberia. He began, in fact, to hate Mexico and Mexicans when he attended a cockfight and was repelled by the rites surrounding the cock's death. Too much fake mummery to enoble the cock's death.

In partial explanation for his reaction to Mexico, Greene acknowledges he was depressed by the difficult journey. Furthermore, the loss of his glasses had caused him severe eye strain and added to the depression that colored his judgment. He seems, however, not to have suffered from impaired vision when it came to assessing the political and religious situation.

Greene found the churches destroyed and priests banished in Tabasco. In Chiapas, the churches remained but were not to be used for religious purposes. Priests were outlawed but Masses were celebrated nonetheless in private rooms and in hushed tones. Greene's most famous novel, *The Power and the Glory* (1940), entitled the *Labyrinthine Ways* in the United States, was to be inspired by this unhappy situation. Before that, however, an extraordinary travel book resulted: *The Lawless Roads* (1939) not only details a journey engrossing in itself but shows the genesis of *The Power and the Glory,* and perhaps parts of *Brighton Rock.* And it offers generally an insightful glance into how Greene moves from fact to fiction.

One example might serve to show the raw material Greene transformed into *The Power and the Glory*. The whisky priest can be seen as an amalgam of three or four priests. The primary suggestion is probably Father Miguel Pro, who returned to Mexico as a newly ordained Jesuit in 1926 during President Calles' fierce persecution of religion. Pro travelled in mufti, said Mass, heard confessions, gave Communion for a year and a half before his capture and execution. Once, like Greene's fictional priest, he even escaped when his captors had him in their hands. The incident, however, points up the difference in Father Pro and Greene's priest. Pro was a consummate actor and escaped capture by posing to the police as a plain-clothes detective. He seems genuinely stronger than the fictional priest, and neither fathered a child nor suffered from alcoholism.

The other suggestions came from the disreputable but kindly Father Rey, who had a wife and child, also from a bishop who was reported to have fathered a child, and most especially from an unnamed priest, the last one in Tabasco, who fled over the border to Chiapas because the people were afraid to protect him. Though not known to have fathered any children, he was a whisky priest who once, while drunk, insisted on baptizing a boy Brigitta (the name Greene used for the daughter of his whisky priest). Suggestions for other characters, incidents, and of course settings are many in *The Lawless Roads*. However, the reader can glean even from this brief exposure to the book insights into the imaginative process that transformed a difficult journey into an extraordinary novel.

A year before *The Power and the Glory*, Greene published *The Confidential Agent*. Then, with the outbreak of war, he was assigned to Secret Intelligence Service, or MI6, as it is called. In 1942, he came under the authority of Kim Philby, the notorious spy who defected to Russia, and he was assigned the same year to special duties in Sierra Leone, West Africa. Philby did not remember much that Greene was able to accomplish in Africa but recalled clearly a meeting to discuss Greene's proposal to use a roving brothel. How better frustrate the French and Germans suspected of spying on British shipping in Portugese Guiana![2] As for Greene's memories of Philby, his affection and admiration for the idealism and kindliness of this double agent are detailed in his essay, "The Spy," in *Collected Essays*: "I saw the beginning of this affair [Philby's attempt to organize an efficient section for his purposes]—indeed I resigned rather than accept the promotion which was one tiny cog in the machinery of his intrigue. I attributed it then to a personal drive for power, the only characteristic in Philby which I thought disagreeable. I am glad now that I was wrong. He was serving a cause and not himself, and so my old liking for him comes back."

As Greene saw it, Philby had found a faith in Communism, and he would not junk it because it had been abused by Stalin, anymore than loyal Catholics would junk a faith abused by Inquisitors or the Roman Curia. If Maurice Castle of *The Human Factor* owes anything to Philby, it is the belief that there are higher loyalties than that to one's country.

In the next five years, Greene wrote his last two explicitly religious novels: *The Heart of the Matter* (1948) and *The End of the Affair* (1951); a novel written for the screen, *The Third Man* (1950); and a book of essays, *The Lost Childhood and Other Essays* (1951). The title essay of the latter is one of the four most revealing bits of autobiography Greene has given us, the others being the two travel books and the autobiography itself.

Greene tells here of his own decision to be a writer when at fourteen years of age he read Marjorie Bowen's *Viper of Milan*. Why was this book so influential? It gave him a subject matter—evil. "Goodness has only once found a perfect incarnation in a human body and never will again, but evil can always find a home there. Human nature is not black and white but black and grey." He found there too the "sense of doom that lies over success—the feeling that the pendulum is about to swing." This sense, he tells us, he could have found in Greek literature had he known the classics. One might think in reading the essay, he were reading the young Thomas Hardy, and to a point the novelists have much in common.

This sense of evil, then, came to Greene in his early reading, long before any religious experience could explain it. He has said elsewhere that early reading is much more formative than early religious education, and this essay bears out that belief. He concludes with a passage from the Irish poet "A.E." that he is fond of quoting:

In ancient shadows and twilights
Where childhood had strayed,
The world's great sorrows were born
And its heroes were made.
In the lost boyhood of Judas
Christ was betrayed.

In 1952 Greene was invited to the United States to receive the Catholic Literary Award for *The End of the Affair*. In that shameful era of McCarthyism, Greene was initially denied a visa by the McCarran Act because he had, during a few undergraduate weeks, belonged to the Communist Party. He was cleared after three days and allowed in. Later in the year he applied again for a second visa and was put through red tape for more than a month. Finally he decided not to come.

The difficulty with the second trip stemmed from an open letter to Charley Chaplin. Chaplin had been asked and had agreed to appear before the House Committee on Un-American Activities and then subsequently had been told he need not appear. When, however, he left for Europe for the filming of *Limelight*, he was cabled that he could not return to the country unless he was willing to answer charges against his personal character and political beliefs. Chaplin never returned to this country until finally Hollywood offered him a special Academy Award in 1972. Greene's letter came to the defense of Chaplin and suggested he satirize the House Committee on Un-American Activities in a film in which his Tramp appeared before them.[3]

These difficulties in visiting the States together with his objections to the American policy in Vietnam that he saw as a reporter are in large measure responsible for the anti-Americanism so many have noted in Greene. Perhaps one other earlier issue also played its part. In 1938, while in Mexico, Greene learned he was being sued for libel by Shirley Temple because of a movie review he had written in *Night and Day*. In this 1937 review of *Wee Willie Winkie*, Greene suggested that the child's appeal was not primarily her acting but an insidiously prurient appeal that allowed old men to enjoy her for reasons they would not admit to themselves. The suit was settled out of court and ruined the struggling publication. John Atkins believes that Hollywood film moguls probably "came to a collective if informal decision that Greene must be stopped" [4] for his negative reviews of American films and seized upon this opportunity when it came. In any event, one can see that Greene's real, if exaggerated, anti-Americanism has some cause. His many journeys as a reporter to various countries under American influence have not assuaged his feelings. In particular, American interest in supporting any "third force," however corrupt or vicious, in preference to Communism does not appeal to a man who admires Castro but who despised the Haitian dictator, "Papa Doc" Duvalier.

Greene published two novels in 1955, *Loser Takes All* and *The Quiet American*. The former shows the beginning of a new development in Greene, one that brings humor to the forefront. Greene's novels and stories have always had humorous elements, but never has humor dominated as it does in two later novels, *Our Man in Havana* (1958) and *Travels With My Aunt* (1969), as well as in his third and fifth plays, *The Complaisant Lover* (1959) and *The Return of A. J. Raffles* (1976) or in many of the stories in *May We Borrow Your Husband* (1967).

*The Comedians* (1966) was Greene's first novel in five years, and he wrote only three more in the next twelve years: *Travels With My Aunt* (1969), *The Honorary Consul* (1973), and *The Human Factor* (1978). While this might be a goodly number for another novelist, readers had come to expect more frequent novels from Greene. Perhaps age has slowed him down slightly. He confessed to V. S. Pritchett that he writes only half as many words each day as he used to. Nonetheless, Greene has not noticeably slowed down so much as he has turned to other genres than the novel.

I mentioned above that Greene has cut his daily word production in half. A glance at his method of composition will prove interesting. He writes 200 words every morning, then corrects in great detail in the evening. Unlike Ernest Hemingway, Greene has no liking for the typewriter. He dictates his corrected manuscript into the tape recorder and eventually sends the tapes from his home in Antibes to England, where they will be typed and returned.[5] His more remote preparation is one he learned after his second and third novels, *The Name of Action* and *Rumour at Nightfall*, proved so unsuccessful that Greene himself eventually suppressed them. From that time, Greene discovered that he needs first to have known his characters and his situations and then to have forgotten them. He cannot mentally photograph his characters. They must emerge as an amalgam of bits and pieces of other characters he has known and forgotten if they are to be true. His action must be life which has been sufficiently forgotten that he cannot recognize it when it again emerges. Otherwise he is reporting and not creating. He does of course sketch his plot out but incidents are added and characters appear and reappear in a way he cannot anticipate. A novelist must forget. "What he forgets is the compost of the imagination."

Thus the same compost can serve quite different stories. In *The Human Factor* (1978), Maurice Castle drops and receives espionage notes in a tree trunk because as a youth he had exchanged love notes with a young girl that way. This method of exchanging notes with a girl had been anticipated many years earlier in a story called "The Innocent " (1937). Also Castle's situation as a double spy, with the Russians whisking him out of the country in the nick of time, had been anticipated in a very early story, "I Spy," in which a young boy sees his father being whisked out of the country forever while the father assumes his son is asleep. Since this story was written in 1930, one will see how erroneous it is to assume *The Human Factor* is based on Kim Philby's defection to Russia in 1963.

Similar incidents can occur in stories closer together than the two mentioned above. The double suicide pact in *Brighton Rock* (1938) appeared a year earlier in a story called "A Drive in the Country." Thus, Greene does not consciously set aside an incident to be used much later. It comes, as in a dream, of itself, and when it surfaces appropriately he uses it. Surely some parts of his friend Philby's defection surfaced when the author was writing *The Human Factor.* Greene speaks in *A Sort of Life* of the writer's need to use even the suffering of others, when he tells us "there is a splinter of ice in the heart of a writer." He must endure pain, his own and others', because he may one day need to draw on the experience.

Greene retired as a director of Bodley Head in 1968, a position he had held ten years. He lives in Antibes on the French Riviera except during "the season." He rarely goes to England, almost never to the United States, but continues to travel to every other part of the world. He has visited Castro in Cuba, Torrijos in Panama, and the late Ho Chi Minh in Vietnam. He has journeyed to South Africa, Israel, Dahomey, Sweden, Istanbul, Argentina, Czechoslovakia and on and on. Despite the reductive label critics have applied to his settings — Greeneland — Greene's novels have many more and varied settings than those of almost any novelist who comes to mind. And the settings are authentic.

The facts of Greene's life, then, help elucidate the origin of his dominant fictional themes. We have in the preface alluded to the causes of his major obsession with the divided self, with betrayal, with suicide, with evil. We find in his life some explanation not only for these but for other recurring themes: boredom, lost childhood, religious doubt, suffering's value, flight, espionage, higher loyalties than patriotism, and anti-Americanism. Since "forgotten" details from life are the acknowledged "compost" of his imagination, the reader will do well to be aware of that compost at the outset of this study. Such awareness will enable him to see how unrelenting Greene's themes have been over so long a writing career.

## Chapter Two

## *THE MAN WITHIN* (1929)

Graham Greene's first novel, *The Man Within*, concerns a divided self. "There's another man within me that's angry with me,"[1] reads the motto from Sir Thomas Browne, and the reader familiar with Greene's mature work finds in this novel a literary talent that is itself divided. Present are the later thematic concerns: betrayal of a friend, fearful flight from pursuers, suicide justified by love for another, and the suffering from a too tender conscience. Present too are Greene's ability to tell a fast-moving tale, his opening in the middle of things and supplying background information later, his ability to make certain scenes—like the courtroom scene—come vividly alive, his use of light and dark for atmosphere and for thematic effect, his achieving symbolic resonances from biblical or fairy-tale allusions that repeat themselves and enhance the theme, and his nicely wrought structure, opening in escape that is not escape and concluding ironically in capture and death that are true escape. Absent notably are Greene's later skill in handling, or skirting, a love scene without embarrassing sentimentality, his gift for suggesting setting vividly and meaningfully without lengthy descriptive passages, and his ability to convey subtle internal conflict without having to externalize such conflict in allegorical fashion.

The story is set in the early nineteenth century. As it opens Francis Andrews flees a group of fellow whisky smugglers he has betrayed to the authorities. He is harbored by a young woman, Elizabeth, who will eventually pay with her life for having helped him. In the meantime, however, she brings out the best in the cowardly Andrews, convincing him to give testimony against the smugglers, who have killed an excise man. In his testimony, he is never certain whether he acts for Elizabeth or for Lucy, an attractive, promiscuous mistress of the chief prosecutor, who has offered herself to Andrews in return for his help in the trial.

The two women clearly depict the two sides of young Andrews' divided self. Lucy, of course, represents the flesh at its most appealing, Elizabeth the spirit. Andrews has too long let the former dominate, showing cowardice, selfishness, and fear for his life. Nevertheless, there is evidence of the other self within. He has been a sensitive and loving son to his mother, has tried with some great effort to please his father, and shows himself capable not only of reciprocating Elizabeth's goodness and love, but eventually of displaying a new-found courage and independence.

The trial's testimony over, Andrews vacillates as usual when trying to decide about Lucy's favors. Finally, he allows himself to be seduced and returns laden with guilt to Elizabeth so that he might warn her that the smugglers intend to avenge themselves on her. However, Elizabeth's belief in God and in the hereafter leave her unafraid about the possibility of her death, and she refuses to flee.

When Andrews leaves the cottage to get water, she is killed. Andrews had heard screams, but he fearfully ran for help rather than run to the cottage. Now he blames himself and poses to the police as her killer. He thus makes amends for the betrayal of Carlyon, his friend and leader of the smugglers, who is now free to escape. He tells what he believes to be the truth since he blames Elizabeth's death on his cowardice. He performs a heroic act, compensating for his previous cowardice, a cowardice planted and nourished in him by a vigorous but insensitive father, who despised him. Thus the love and courage awakened in Andrews by Elizabeth, who did not despise him, had brought his two selves together and made him capable of something other than a selfish, cowardly act. As the novel concludes, Andrews is about to take his own life.

The novel's main thesis is, of course, the need to bring together the divided self, what might be called spiritual and fleshly concerns. Andrews recognized early the brute that his father was but nonetheless could not free himself of the need to prove himself in his father's terms. His education in Latin and Greek meant nothing to his father but an opportunity to boast of his son; his gathering flowers with his mother did not even have that value; and, in a painful scene, the father tears their pressed leaves out of an album. When his father dies and Carlyon offers him an opportunity to join the crew of *The Good Chance*, Andrews seizes it. School, he has been made to feel, is worthless, and Carlyon appeals to his romantic side. He will prove his mettle in the very way his father proved himself, and thus he allows his father to get a still stronger hold on him.

Andrews' subsequent failure to measure up to his father as a seaman further embitters and divides him. One half of him knows his father's values are worthless, but the other side still nags him to prove himself a man like his father. Though Carlyon substitutes as a father, he is no help since his kindness does not remove Andrews' internal critic. Furthermore, Carlyon himself provides no model because he is not a whole man. He loves the beautiful because he himself is physically ugly, "The man was only a romantic fool with an ugly face. That was the real secret of his humility, his courage, even his love of beauty. He was always seeking a compensation for his face, as though an ape in ermine were less an ape." Thus Carlyon proves a thoroughly amoral man. His actions are based merely on his esthetics.

Elizabeth, then, is the first person Andrews comes to know whose inner self is not divided. When Carlyon first comes to her cottage, he himself is surprised by her:

> "You cannot be mixed up in this. You don't belong to our world, noise, hate. Stay with peace."
> "Are the two so separate?" she asked.
> He listened with his head a little on one side and eyes half closed, like a man in the presence of a faint music. Then he covered his eyes for a moment with his hand.
> "You muddle me," he said.
> "Are they so separate?"she repeated.
> "Let them remain separate,"he said vehemently and bitterly.

Unlike Elizabeth, Andrews' parents had also divided selves. His father had been a swashbuckling hero on ship but an insensitive tyrant in the home. His mother's excessively romantic side had made her succumb to the suggestion she elope with the senior Andrews. Carlyon was the only other major influence in Andrews' life until he met Elizabeth. Thus it is ironic that Andrews achieves some measure of wholeness or integrity when he "kills" Elizabeth. Yet that is what happens. His failure to return immediately to the cottage when he knows it has been broken into does indeed result in Elizabeth's death, and his accepting blame for that death demonstrates a courage and a love he has not before shown. As a result, he transcends the timid and self-critical person his father's bullying has made him. Moreover his life offering is not only for Elizabeth (his spiritual half) but for Carlyon (his father-dominated or fleshly half), who is now free. Thus, he expiates the betrayal and shows a bravery by other standards than his father's, finally freeing himself of that domination.

A theme that Greene is to use so dramatically twenty years later, in *The Heart of the Matter*, is found here in his first novel. I refer to suicide motivated by love of another. In this novel, Elizabeth stabs herself with Andrews' knife when she fears she will give him away as Carlyon's man brutalizes her. The description of this action is simple and straightforward and its justification is assumed. In the later novel, it will be central to the story, and its justification or lack of justification will be presented in the light of Catholic theology. However, even in his first novel, this young Catholic convert seems implicitly to play with an idea he will later make explicit, the "virtue of disloyalty." Because of the strong disapproval of suicide in Catholic moral theology, Greene poses as "a protestant in a Catholic society." In an address delivered at the University of Hamburg in 1969, Greene contended:

> The writer is driven by his own vocation to be a protestant in a Catholic society, a catholic in a Protestant one, to see the virtues of the capitalist in a Communist society, of the communist in a Capitalist state. . . . He stands for the victims, and the victims change. Loyalty confines you to accepted opinions: loyalty forbids you to comprehend sympathetically your dissident fellows; but disloyalty encourages you to roam through any human mind; it gives the novelist an extra dimension of understanding.[2]

Greene's sympathetic treatment of suicide is an early effort to play the role of devil's advocate. Later his efforts will prove more explicit.

Another major theme of several later novels is seen here too in the betrayal of a friend. Andrews betrays Carlyon as Scobie will later betray his faithful servant Ali in *The Heart of the Matter* or as Castle will betray his country in *The Human Factor*.

One can see, then, in the young Greene a concern for certain themes, that will dominate his view of life and that will be more thoroughly incorporated into his later fiction. These are what Allott and Farris have called the "obsessions" that make a writer a poet and not just a journeyman in fiction.[3]

Among the fictional techniques that Greene employs in his first novel and will use repeatedly in his later works is the epic device of beginning *in medias res* and, having thus begun in the middle, of returning later by flashback for necessary exposition. Thus we do not learn of Andrews' nor of Elizabeth's background until the fifth chapter. This device has the effect of involving us immediately in the story. We can open with a suspenseful escape scene.

Furthermore, Greene thereby structures the novel on an irony that helps convey his meaning. It both opens and closes with escape. Andrews flees from Carlyon but also flees from himself. He had betrayed the smugglers not from moral indignation but because they did not respect him as they did his father. At story's end, when they catch up with him, he finds, as we have seen, true escape from the shadow of his father that has so dominated him.

Greene employs symbolic resonances in the same manner he will so effectively use in later books. Four allusions are made to Hansel and Gretel, and of course the two children struggling against the witch in the ginger-bread house in the woods quite obviously parallel Andrews and

Elizabeth in their cottage trying to hide from Carlyon. What purpose does such a symbol serve? It enlists the archetypal overtones suggested by all fairy tales, and specifically those suggested by "Hansel and Gretel." Despite young Andrews' rejection by his father, he still tries to please his father, to succeed as his father might wish him to succeed. Bruno Bettleheim says in analyzing Hansel and Gretel that "before a child has the courage to embark on a voyage of finding himself, of becoming an independent person through meeting the world, he can develop initiative only in trying to return to passivity, to secure for himself eternally dependent gratification. 'Hansel and Gretel' tells that this will not work in the long run."[4] Thus young Andrews relives an oft-told tale.

Greene's use of light and dark to aid atmosphere and theme is a technique he will employ in most later novels. Some of these, like *The Honorary Consul* and *The Comedians*, will take place largely in the dark. Since fiction is "felt life," atmosphere and setting serve, of course, to make the reader experience the author's vision and not merely to be told it. They move the reader from what Newman called "notional assent" to a proposition to "real assent." Since so many of Greene's characters are searching, groping, lost characters, darkness is an effective metaphor for their state of mind. Significantly, the only actions in this novel that do not occur in the dark or in the fog are Andrews' testimony at the trial, which occurs in partial light, and his return to Elizabeth after the trial, which occurs in the only golden sunlight we experience in the book.

Absent from this early novel is Greene's skill with a love scene:

> "Come here," Andrews said and when she came he gazed at her with wonder. "To think that I can say come and you'll come. You shouldn't though. I wish you could realize how unworthy I am of you."

The whole scene is embarrassingly sentimental, and sounds like the Victorian "higher love."

> He walked slowly back and stood still in the centre of the room, watching Elizabeth but making no attempt to go to her. "Listen," he said, "it's possible that these men will get me." He spoke dully and apprehensively. "I've always left things too late, so I want to tell you now that I love you as I've never loved anyone or anything in the world before. Even myself. I was a blind fool this afternoon to quarrel in these few certain hours. I'm sorry. I think I'm beginning to understand. I'll ask for you only when we're married and that as a favor which I don't

> deserve. You were right. You are holy. I don't see how I can ever touch you without soiling you a little, but my God," his voice became vehement and he took a step towards her, " I'll serve you, how I'll serve you."

The reader is almost driven to something like "The Miller's Tale" to find relief from these courtly love scenes that dominate the chapter. And there is no reason to suppose this romantic excess anymore appropriate to the characters in this novel than it would be to similar characters in later novels. Yet the sentimentality contrasts sharply with the deftly handled love scenes of *The End of the Affair* or *The Comedians*, or any later novel.

Absent from this novel too is Greene's ability to make a reader experience something without his insistence on it. Early in the novel, Andrews explains why he came to the cottage:

> "It was only fear that made me come. You other people never seem to understand fear. You expect everyone to be brave like yourself. It's not a man's fault whether he's brave or cowardly. It's all in the way he's born. My father and mother made me. I didn't make myself."

It is much too early in the novel for Andrews' actions to have convinced us he is a coward. Thus, we sense the author's ventriloquism. Greene is directing our thinking and making his character wear his cowardice like a badge. We are not convinced. For a writer whose style is so precise in his later works, this scene and others call attention to themselves. Another stylistic infelicity not to be found in later Greene is an occasional lack of specificity, "He described what he would do to her in a brief, physiological sentence, and rejoiced at the flush which it fetched to her face."

Finally, the internal struggle of his protagonist is something that would remain internal in a later Scobie or Sarah Miles. In this early novel, Greene is forced to externalize as in allegory. Andrews' spiritual half is Elizabeth, his fleshly half, Lucy. Rather than do a good thing for a bad reason, Andrews does a good thing for a bad *person*, Lucy, or does he really do it for a good person, Elizabeth? Greene seems not yet able to deal with subtle, internal motivation and thus he externalizes in a manner that seems bad Hawthorne.

Nevertheless, most of Greene's talents and themes are present in this first novel, at least *in ovo*. To say this is not to say that he wrote almost as good a novel as some of his later ones but merely to say that *The Man Within* is a substantial achievement for a first novel and sets a pattern that will be improved upon.

## Chapter Three

## *ENGLAND MADE ME* (1935)

Between *The Man Within* and *England Made Me*, Greene wrote four novels. Two of these, *The Name of Action* (1930) and *Rumour at Nightfall* (1931), he later removed from his canon. These disappointing novels were followed by the very successful *Stamboul Train* (1934), published in the United States as *Orient Express,* and by *It's A Battlefield* (1934). Then one year later Greene wrote perhaps his finest novel to that time, as well as one of his personal favorites, *England Made Me*.

Set in Sweden, a country Greene had not visited until he fixed upon his story, *England Made Me* deals with an incestuous love between brother and sister. Kate and Anthony Farrant are English exiles in a larger group of spiritual exiles, who steal a livelihood, as Kate puts it, and give nothing in return. In a sense, then, the illicit and unfruitful relationship of Kate and Anthony becomes emblematic of the relationship of all the characters to their setting.

As the novel opens in a Stockholm bar, Kate waits, like a jilted lover, for Anthony. He has lost still another job, and she is anxious to keep him with her by getting him a job at Krogh's. A word from her to Eric Krogh, to whom she is both secretary and mistress, secures Anthony the job with this powerful industrialist. He will serve as Krogh's body guard since the only talent this easygoing drifter has is pistol marksmanship.

Anthony shortly weans Krogh away from operas that he does not enjoy and takes him to bars that he does. However, Kate is not to have her beloved brother with her or the firm very long; two elements interfere. One is Anthony's moral objection to illegal investments in which he discovers Krogh is involved, and the other is an attachment Anthony develops for a visiting English tourist, Lucia Davidge. Lucia concludes her vacation and returns home, and Anthony wishes to follow. However, before he can, Krogh's terrier-like protector, Fred Hall, returns to Stockholm. Having discovered Anthony's potentially destructive knowledge of Krogh's investments, Hall murders Anthony in the fog, and throws his body in the river. The novel ends with the scene at Anthony's funeral. Minty, another displaced Englishman, acquaintance of Anthony's and full-time reporter assigned to watch Krogh, taunts Hall about the service he renders to Krogh. However, Kate is passive. She indicates she is leaving Krogh's and just moving on, disappointed that the telepathy she had enjoyed with her twin brother was no longer there when Anthony's life was in danger.

Perhaps what first strikes Greene's readers is how he has improved his craft since *The Man Within*. The style is patently better and the method less melodramatic. Even the stream of consciousness, though at times appearing dated to a current reader, serves Greene well. He uses it, for example, to blend Kate's thoughts of Eric, as she lies next to him, with her thoughts of Anthony whom she really loves and for whom she uses Eric. Her thoughts of Anthony also fuse with thoughts of herself.

The literary allusions that Greene enjoys for their symbolic assistance are here used in greater measure and, for the most part, more implicitly. Least implicit, but nonetheless effective, is the allusion to Blake's "Tiger." Anthony wins a toy tiger at a shooting gallery. Later Kate thinks of Anthony as the "Tiger burning bright in Tivoli, immortal eye," and then he blends into Eric who sleeps next to her. She refers to her "twisted sinews of the heart" and then, thinking mostly of Anthony and of herself:

> Don't be afraid. Don't hesitate. No cause of fear.
> No bulls on this exchange. The tiger bright. The forests.
> Sleep. Our bond. The new redemption. And we rise, we
> rise. And God who made the lamb made Whitaker, made
> Lowenstein. "But you are Lucky." Hammond said that day
> in Leather Lane, "Krogh's safe. Whatever comes or goes
> people will always everywhere have to buy Krogh's." The
> market steady. The Strand, the water and a street between
> us. Sleep. The new redemption. No bulls, the tiger and
> the lamb. The bears. The forests. Sleep. The stock is
> sound. The closing price. We rise.

What is suggested throughout the novel, is the need for Anthony to convert himself to a tiger in these risky, dangerous, financial "forests of the night" that are Krogh's empire. Later, when Anthony gives his toy tiger to his English girlfriend, Lucia, we have a possible allusion to Anthony being left as a lamb of "innocence" in this world of "experience." This seems a more subtle version of *The Man Within's* "divided self" theme: one must be tiger as well as lamb in the world of Whitaker, Lowenstein, and Krogh.

The opera to which Anthony is obliged to take Krogh is apparently *Tristan und Isolde*, and the love potion, the tragic triangle of Tristan, Isolde and Marc, and the fatal black sails, are not without their parallel in the love triangle of Anthony, Kate, and Eric. This is not an explicit symbol, but there are sufficient tragic resonances of the one story to lend effect to the other.

The most elaborate literary allusion that serves the same purpose is that from *Pericles*. Krogh offers to support Prof. Hammarsten's production of his own translation of Shakespeare's play. The play involves incest as does *England Made Me*. Yet Anthony is not equated with the incestuous Antiochus so much as he is with the moral Gower whom Shakespeare, or the unknown author of *Pericles*, uses as a choral commentator. Anthony, more lamb than tiger, is the voice of conscience throughout *England Made Me*, and Kate, more tiger than lamb, is critical of the "good looks and conscience" that are the "flower of our class." She resents having encouraged Anthony back to public school where he acquired his conscience.

Anthony, of course, is not quite moral Gower and he has even lost a position for lining his own pockets and not just his employer's, but, he rightly contends, "There are things I won't do." One of those things is to support Krogh's illegal use of funds from one company to bolster depleted resources of another. Still more, he will not condone Krogh's firing of old Andersson once Krogh has talked this employee out of leading a strike nor will he be a party to Krogh's having young Andersson beaten up and thrown out of the restaurant when this innocent comes to his employer, Krogh, about the "mistake" over his loyal father's firing. Anthony's conscience brings about his own murder. Thus at his funeral we are meant to see him as moral Gower when Prof. Hammarsten's condolences to Kate and his remarks about the progress of *Pericles* are joined, "Poor young man. A week too in the water. . . . The rehearsals are going well. All except Gower. I need Gower."

The method of structuring this novel is one that Greene brings to perfection in later novels. Within a brief story he not only has seven parts, but as many as four or five chapters within these parts. The effect of this technique is that the short scenes suggest more than can be said. The author can be brief yet allusive, and the reader moves in a world that is, as a result, larger and more complex. Another effect of the method is that the author can avoid direct comment by juxtaposing scenes that comment on each other. This method we will see at its best when we discuss *The Human Factor*. Yet even in this early novel our knowledge of the main characters is rounded by having Kate's opening chapter reflections on her brother joined to the second chapter's interior monologue of Anthony. Perhaps a better example is to be found in Part V, which presents young Andersson as he leaves for Stockholm to speak with Mr. Krogh, who used to be a laborer himself, followed by a scene in which Kate and Anthony drive Krogh to a party that is to celebrate the announcement of Kate's and Krogh's wedding. In this scene, Krogh stops the car to talk to workmen who are constructing a bridge, as he used to, but he does not succeed in having the laborers recognize him as "one of them." In the third scene, a plane brings the callous but dedicated Fred Hall to Stockholm to assist his employer. His character is dramatized by his smoking in the restroom to the danger of all the passengers. Finally the last scene offers a grand party in which all the characters are brought together and which ends when Anthony refuses to get rid of young Andersson for Krogh. The young man has come up to the city merely for a few polite words with his employer. Krogh ought to see him, Anthony believes. Fred Hall appears, sizes up the situation, and beats Andersson up with brass knuckles.

So much is offered dramatically in a few pages: the loyal young laborer who believes in Krogh's because it's run by a former laborer; Krogh's callousness to his workers as evidenced when he mistreats young Andersson as he had mistreated his father before him; Fred Hall's savage, unreasoning protection of his employer's remoteness; Krogh's deep-seated desire to be one of the people he has cut himself off from; and Anthony's loyalty to his employer "up to a point." Anthony's refusal to get rid of Andersson and the look of surprise on Andersson's bloody face are the closest we come to comment on the action.

The method is, of course, tied up with point of view since Greene not only juxtaposes scenes but shifts his focal point from one character to another. He uses the method he learned from Henry James, employing third person rather than first person, thereby involving his center of focus himself or herself in the dramatic action. Thus we have more perspective on the person who is providing the focus.

The technique works well as the reader gets inside and behind all of the major characters, though the primary foci remain Anthony and Kate. Nevertheless, critics have attributed to Greene ideas that he clearly intends for his characters partly because he employs third person rather than first. It is essential to understand that when Greene writes, "For he was hopelessly lost in the world of business that she knew so well, the world where she was at home: he had a child's cunning in a world of cunning men: he was dishonest, but he was not dishonest enough," that this is Kate's judgment, not Greene's. As Greene perfects his use of Jamesian point of view in later novels, the chances for such error seem greater. For example, when Greene writes in his chapter on Fred Hall, "She was a skirt, she only lived with Krogh, he was convinced, for what she could get out of him," he would very likely have left out the parenthetical, "was convinced," in later novels. The confusion over who is speaking has occurred often enough to annoy Greene and to have him reply to hostile critics. But we will discuss this matter further when we look at *The Quiet American*.

The influence of Henry James will also be seen in Greene 's economy and sparseness of authorial comment. He does, to use Percy Lubbock's expression, "surround facts" rather than walk directly up to them.

Greene's development of his characters has progressed significantly since *The Man Within*. He believes Kate Farrant is "the woman I have drawn better than any other, with the possible exception of Sarah in *The End of the Affair*," and that seems an accurate assessment. Kate is indeed complex. She is sister, mother and lover to Anthony, has all the practical business acumen he lacks, yet has none of the moral sense he possesses, and this she considers a blessing. Kate is a "tiger" in "the forests of the night." She is sufficiently hard-headed and amoral to survive Krogh's financial jungle. Still her whole life centers around Anthony, and because he proves a lamb, she is shorn as well as he. Greene manages to convey both her independence and her vulnerability, her love for her brother and her physical indifference to anyone else. Yet though she does not love Krogh, she cares for him, is protective of him even against her brother. When Krogh wants to marry her to guarantee her not testifying in court against him, she appreciates the crude honesty of the proposal and agrees. Still she assures him he could have counted on her loyalty without marriage. She is indeed the best depicted woman in Greene's early fiction.

Anthony too represents a development in characterization since young Andrews of *The Man Within*. As merely the cavalier ne'er-do-well, he would have been something of a type, but he transcends the type. He shows more conscience than any other character. He loves his sister but without reciprocating so clearly a sexual love as she has for him. At least he ultimately chooses the sexual love he can have with Lucia over the platonic love to which he is limited with Kate. Thus in her jealous frustration, Kate strikes at his outstretched hand with her pen knife.

Despite his conscience on more important matters, on lesser matters Anthony lies constantly to himself and to others. Of course, he is only telling others tall tales, but he has done so for so long that he rarely looks at himself, rarely sees himself as Kate sees him. There is one scene on a park bench where for a moment he surprises Kate by what seems self-knowledge, "I haven't a future, Kate." Then he undoes this insight in Micawber-like fashion, "'Of course,' he said 'the luck may turn. Something may turn up.' She recognized at once that the moment had passed. . . . It had been less self-knowledge than a temporary break in the cloud of self-deception."

Part of what makes Anthony an intriguing character is his seediness. It is a quality that still another of the novel's characters, Minty, has to an even greater extent, and a quality that Greene makes much of from now on in his novels, though he has grown to dislike the term. One reason seediness may interest Greene is because it is so obvious a metaphor for a state of mind and soul. It serves such a purpose in Anthony and even more so in Minty. This Harrovian is Greene's seedy character *par excellence*. He lives in a dirty flat, keeps a spider under his tooth glass (something that grows into a symbol for all the estranged characters in the novel), trails in his absurdly long black coat through rainy streets, looking for any newsworthy story about Krogh. And he practices his Anglo-Catholicism in a pathetic way, even praying God for the destruction of his enemies.

A year later Greene was to discover a more fundamental reason that the seedy appealed to him. After journeying through the heart of Liberia to the coastal city of Monrovia, Greene tells us in *Journey Without Maps* that he found Europeans who had perhaps never gotten to the interior of Liberia, to the communal life of the natives, with its terror and its gentleness. Still, in the seediness of Monrovia, they were closer than we to the central darkness. "This may explain the deep appeal of the seedy. It *is* nearer the beginning; like Monrovia its building has begun wrong, but at least it has only begun; it hasn't reached so far away as the smart, the new, the chic, the cerebral."

As Greene has acknowledged, Minty becomes too large for *England Made Me*. Useful to the plot in showing up the sham qualities of Anthony, who wears a Harrow tie without having attended Harrow and useful too as a central personification of the seediness all the characters share, he does nevertheless take over. Greene gives more time and attention to him than to any other character apart from Kate and Anthony. He allows most of Part III and Part VII to be seen from Minty's point of view, including the final scene, which might more properly have been Kate's. Nonetheless, Minty is a well-drawn character. His devotion to Harrow and to the trappings of religion are convincing. His apartment is the real thing, nauseating us as much as it does Anthony and Lucia when they make love there. And if Kate's having the last scene could have rounded out the book in more symmetrical fashion, still Minty can in that scene press Hall about the murder or about his "devotion to Krogh" more easily than could Kate. He is a successful character.

Greene's other characters are drawn just well enough to meet the needs of the story. Watchdog that he is, Hall is not complex and need not be. His loyalty to Krogh is unwavering and he will viciously attack anyone who threatens his employer. Andersson comes nicely to life as we see him in one chapter leave his machine job, shyly tell his housemate's wife he is going up to Stockholm, and chat with the old lady on the train. He is sufficiently realized for his small but crucial part, just enough for us to feel for him as he is confused and beaten by Hall. Krogh, while not quite coming through as do Anthony and Kate, is perhaps well enough rounded for the remote employer he tends to be. Had we been able to see him at Anthony's funeral and perhaps in the latter part of the novel as we did in his earlier scenes with Anthony, he might have emerged as a truly memorable character. Instead he fades out.

*England Made Me* shows, then, that Greene has improved his fiction-writing skills since *The Man Within* primarily because of his improved characterization, but also because of what he has been learning to do with structure and point of view. Moreover, his love scenes have grown noticeably more authentic and less sentimental. He was ready now to write the major novels that would earn his reputation as "the most accomplished of English novelists."[1]

## Chapter Four

## *BRIGHTON ROCK* (1938)

*Brighton Rock* was the first of Greene's four religious novels. The series was to make him known, to his annoyance, as a Catholic novelist, and, in defense against the label, Greene in his introduction to the Collected Edition of *Brighton Rock* quotes Newman's *Idea of a University*, "I say from the nature of the case, if Literature is to be made a study of human nature, you cannot have a Christian Literature. It is a contradiction in terms to attempt a sinless Literature of sinful man."

Greene does not of course write a sinless literature about sinful man. What he does do for the first time is to use explicitly theological matter to flesh out his theory of the "virtue of disloyalty," a theory we discussed in Chapter Two. In these four novels, that disloyalty takes the form of the author's playing the "protestant in a Catholic society." Later, in *The Human Factor* or *Our Man in Havana*, he will pose as the communist in a Capitalist state.

To be such a devil's advocate in *Brighton Rock*, Greene takes his Catholic protagonist, makes him as vicious as he makes any character in his entire canon, yet demonstrates that Catholic moral law cannot condemn him, cannot finally know "the appalling strangeness of the mercy of God."

The novel opens with Fred Hale's unsuccessful attempt to escape the protection-racket gang now headed by seventeen-year-old Pinkie Brown. Fred Hale has betrayed the gang's former boss, Kite, to its new, sophisticated competitor, Colleoni. Only by avenging Kite can Pinkie assume real control of men many years his seniors and compete with Colleoni. Pinkie succeeds, though Hale actually dies of a heart attack when the gang attempts to strangle him. Because Hale has technically died of natural causes, Pinkie and his men are not implicated in the death, except perhaps by two loose ends they have left.

One loose end takes the buxom form of Ida Arnold, who was picked up by Hale and who was then surprisingly abandoned when she left Hale to go to the rest room. The papers reported his accidental death, and the police seemed satisfied with that explanation. Ida, however, is not and begins her own relentless search for "poor Fred's murderer." The other loose end is young Rose, who noticed one of Pinkie's men pretending to be Fred Hale and hiding leaflets as part of a newspaper publicity job in which Fred was engaged. Pinkie had arranged to have Fred's remaining leaflets delivered to confuse the police about the time of his death. Rose notices the man, Pinkie looks her up, courts her, and eventually even marries her to keep her from testifying.

From this point, the action of the novel involves both Pinkie's attempts to cover all his traces, an attempt that requires further murder, and Ida's attempt to birddog Pinkie, thus avenging Hale and rescuing Rose. Ida ultimately prevails when Pinkie attempts to have Rose commit suicide, an act to be followed—he lies to her— by his own suicide. Ida arrives with the police, Pinkie is splashed with his own bottle of vitriol, and he plunges to his death in the sea. In the final chapter, Rose, apparently pregnant with Pinkie's child, brings her problems to an old priest who attempts to convince her of God's mercy.

Pinkie is one of the best characters Greene had yet depicted. Vicious as he is, with his sadistic razor slashings, his murders to cover murders, his cruelty to Rose, this young tough's guilt is nonetheless extenuated, his amorality rendered somewhat understandable. Pinkie's conscience has not awakened because his imagination has not awakened: "The word murder conveyed no more to him than the word 'box,' 'collar,' 'giraffe'. . . . The imagination hadn't awoken. That was his strength. He couldn't see through other people's eyes, or feel with their nerves."

As with Andrews in *The Man Within*, the explanation for Pinkie's self-destructive character lies in his lost childhood, "In the lost boyhood of Judas, Christ was betrayed." In a parody of Wordsworth's "Intimations Ode," Greene tells us Pinkie came into the world trailing something other than heavenly clouds of his own glory after him: "hell lay about him in his infancy." Wordsworth could say about the child that "heaven lay about him in his infancy," but Greene sees Pinkie in quite opposite terms, "Heaven was a word: hell was something he could trust." Pinkie's vivid memory of his father and mother having sexual intercourse in his presence had turned him from all pleasures of the flesh and tempted him for a while with thoughts of a celibate priesthood.

When Pinkie was seventeen, Kite became a surrogate father to him. Pinkie's lack of conscience, his unconcern for himself, his sadomasochistic tendencies, which early showed themselves as a substitute for thwarted sexual impulse, stood the youth in good stead for a new vocation that required unflinching loyalty, razor slashings, and, if necessary, murder. His corruption was almost guaranteed. To say this is not to reduce the novel from a theological statement to a sociological one in which environment has determined the boy's character. Rose survives somewhat the same circumstances. Pinkie's guilt is extenuated, never excused.

Rose is a prefiguration of the unorthodox "saint" that Greene developed more subtly in his later novels, in the Mexican priest of *The Power and the Glory*, in Sarah Miles of *The End of the Affair*, and to some extent perhaps in Scobie of *The Heart of the Matter*. Like Scobie, Rose wills her damnation out of love. She is not so well drawn as Scobie will be, at times making her naive goodness less credible than his, but she is motivated by selfless concern for another. When she refuses to reject Pinkie or when she chooses to commit suicide (though she cannot go through with it), Rose wants an afterlife with Pinkie. She would rather be damned with him than see him damned alone. "Would he shoot himself alone, without her? Then he would be damned, and she wouldn't have her chance of being damned too, of showing them they couldn't pick and choose." This seems unconvincing until we later hear the old priest cite the actual case of Charles Peguy, who would rather have died in the state of sin than to have believed that a single soul was damned.

If Rose seems naive, we must remember that she is experiencing her first love, that she is more inexperienced than Pinkie, and that she glosses over Pinkie's evil because she believes he returns her love.

The third major character, Ida Arnold, is one of Greene's most successfully depicted women. Carefree as she is, she contrasts with Pinkie in every way, loving the sex he detests and detesting the vicious acts of which he is capable. She believes in no afterlife, neither the hell that absorbs Pinkie's thoughts nor the heaven of which the clergyman speaks at Hale's cremation, a heaven of union with an impersonal One. Since there is no heaven that rewards nor hell that punishes, justice must be sought in the temporal realm. Ida becomes Hale's avenger.

Proponent of a natural, funloving life that is restricted only by her intuitive knowledge of right and wrong, Ida becomes an object of loathing to Rose. The more she dogs Pinkie's steps and the more she tries to rescue Rose, the more the latter is drawn to Pinkie: "I don't care what you've done," "I'd rather be with you than be like her, " she's "not our kind." When Ida tells Rose she is merely trying to spare her suffering, Rose makes the distinction between right and wrong as well as good and evil that is so central to the novel. Ida remarks to Rose:

> "I know one thing you don't. I know the difference between Right and Wrong. They didn't teach you *that* at school."
> Rose didn't answer; the woman was quite right: the two words meant nothing to her. Their taste was extinguished by stronger foods—Good and Evil. The woman could tell her nothing she didn't know about these.

The reader is meant to see the limitations of Ida's natural virtues, the weakness of her self-appropriated role of avenger. Pinkie is more evil than Ida imagines because, as we are told by the old priest, "*Corruptio optimi pessima*," the corruption of the best is the worst. As a Catholic, Pinkie knows the difference between good and evil. Thus his corruption is a greater matter. Yet Ida who is ignorant of the "stronger foods" on which Rose and Pinkie have been fed presumes too much. She is at best a proponent of natural virtue. The world of the supernatural does not exist for her. She has been victimized by a society that has forgotten its primitive roots, its supernatural beliefs. These racial roots and beliefs Greene had rediscovered in his Liberian journey. In place of them, Ida's society had substituted the glitter of a chromium-plated, sinless world and forgotten "the finer taste, the finer pleasure, the finer fear on which we might have built."

The center of focus Greene chooses in the narration of his story alternates between Pinkie and Ida. By choosing such a focus, the author presents his material more dramatically than pictorially. Had he told the story through an omniscient narrator, we might have had a vivid picture but not as much dramatic interaction. Moreover, the theme would, of necessity, have had to be rendered more overtly or didactically. The all-knowing narrator would have directed our thinking. Had the story been told through a first-person narrator, we would perhaps have picked up in the intimacy of self-revelation but lost in drama by not seeing the narrator from the same distance as we see the other characters. Furthermore, no major character in the novel understood himself or the world in which he lived well enough to integrate the same theme into the story. We needed as focus just such a protagonist as Pinkie, desperately in need of God's mercy, and just such an antagonist as Ida, unaware of a merciful God, to create the proper context for the old priest to talk to Rose of the "appalling strangeness of God's mercy."

The victim, Rose, is the center of focus in just two chapters, both in the final section. The first of these allows the reader to see her distinction between right or wrong and good or evil; and it helps the reader understand why, having, out of love, made the choice for evil rather than for good, Rose was not troubled by the lesser distinction between right and wrong. This chapter further prevents the final chapter from seeming a radical break in the book's narration as well as a possible anti-climax to the story.

The final chapter is, of course, crucial. In it Rose visits the old priest in confession, learns of God's mercy and also of the "saintly" Charles Peguy, who like Rose preferred to be damned than to think that a single other person had been damned. Further the final chapter provides as grim an ending as literature can offer. Rose returns home from confession to the two consolations she believes she has left her, the possibility she is carrying Pinkie's baby and the belief that she has a record of Pinkie's love in a phonograph he cut at her insistence. Thus both she and her baby can share Pinkie's love. What the reader knows Pinkie has said on the record and what Rose is doomed to discover is: "God damn you, you little bitch, why can't you go home forever and let me be?"

Greene is effective, if at times obvious, in his use of symbol in *Brighton Rock*. Pinkie carries his private hell in the form of a bottle of vitriol in his back pocket, "Life held the vitriol bottle and warned him: I'll spoil your looks." Then in a symbolically fit conclusion for this self-destructive character, after failing to have Rose kill herself, the vitriol is splashed in his own face, and he plunges to his death in the sea.

Equally obvious but nonetheless effective is the complementary symbol for heaven or the "hound of heaven." Like the narrator in Francis Thompson's poem, Pinkie is pursued by a beast that tries to hold out to him the very thing he seeks by flight, viz. peace. In the final minutes prior to his unsuccessful attempt to have Rose commit suicide and his own successful but unplanned suicide, Pinkie drives with Rose through a heavy rainstorm and imagines this winged beast trying to force its way into his car:

> The car lurched back onto the main road; he turned the bonnet to Brighton. An enormous emotion beat on him; it was like something trying to get in; the pressure of gigantic wings against the glass. *Dona nobis pacem*. He withstood it, with all the bitter force of the school bench, the cement playground, the St. Pancras waiting-room, Dallow's and Judy's secret lust, and the unhappy moment on the pier. If the glass broke, if the beast—whatever it was—got in, God knows what it would do. He had a sense of huge havoc—the confession, the penance and the sacrament—and awful distraction, and he drove blind into the rain. He could see nothing through the cracked stained wind-screen. A bus came upon them and pulled out just in time—he was on the wrong side. He said, suddenly, at random, "We pull in here."

Just as randomly, a few moments later, the words of the Mass' last gospel came to him, "He was in the world and the world was made by Him and the world knew Him not."

The most successful and pervasive symbol may be the setting itself.

Gaudy Brighton Beach contrasts with the grim Nelson Place of Pinkie's childhood and Rose's present. Pinkie wants to escape the Catholic ghetto, Nelson Place, to escape its poverty, the sex scenes of his parents, and his own religious upbringing. However Brighton, symbol of escape, offers no sanctuary but provides instead the glaring light of detection.

Some critics have seen the novel's seven-part structure as a symbolic parody of the seven sacraments.[1] For example, when Pinkie's face is splashed with vitriol in the last section, we have a parody of Extreme Unction, the sacrament of the sick and dying, just as in Part V, his first drink of alcohol and his attempt to lose his virginity are a parody of Holy Orders. The argument for such a structure does not seem equally convincing for all sections. Nonetheless, the reader may form his own conclusion about this ingenious way of reading the novel.

Though the themes of betrayal, of lost childhood, and of the divided self connect *Brighton Rock* with Greene's earliest (and latest) fiction, the novel represents a turning point in Greene's career. From now on he becomes more explicitly a "problem novelist." The term should not be confused with propaganda novelist. Unlike a propaganda novelist, Greene never makes his story subservient to a thesis, but offers the reader a problem or idea that needs working out: Is a thoroughly immoral Pinkie beyond the pale of Christian mercy? (*Brighton Rock*) Are there circumstances in which a man can justifiably betray his country? (*The Human Factor*) Is a country's anti-communism reason enough for a capitalist state to support it? (*The Comedians*) To present such problems and to act as *advocatus diaboli* in any given society will become increasingly Greene's dominating purpose.

Chapter Five

# *THE POWER AND THE GLORY* (1940)

In this second of his religious novels, Greene sets up a metaphorical conflict between the powers of God and the powers of atheism, and between the supernatural order and the natural order. Greene believes in the presence of the former in this world, as the events of the novel may testify. Such a belief is difficult to treat in fiction without running the risk of a scoffing readership. In this novel, however, Greene works more obliquely than in *The End of the Affair* to dramatize the supernatural influence of his unlikely protagonist-saint within the confines of realistic fiction.

The greatness of *The Power and the Glory* lies in Greene's never letting his allegory become a medieval morality play. The forces of good and the forces of evil are not so easily separated. Although his unnamed priest acquires a real holiness through suffering, the author depicts him as a much weaker man than his counterpart, the lieutenant. The latter is not only a strong man, but a good man, who is selflessly devoted to the people. His anti-Catholicism owes its origin to his boyhood memory of a church that did not show a similar concern for its people.

The story is set in deepest Mexico, in the states of Tabasco and Chiapas, which border on Guatemala. Between the revolution in 1910 and the presidency of Camacho in 1940, the country was extremely anti-clerical, and in states like Tabasco and Chiapas religious persecution was severe, as we saw in the first chapter.

We can determine the time frame of the story from a few topical references, such as the one to Sen. Huey Long, as being the 1930s, most likely the time of Greene's visit. For the most part, however, time is ignored for much the same reason that the priest and lieutenant are left unnamed, to suggest that the story concerns every time and every man.

When the story opens, the priest is succumbing to the temptation to leave Mexico. He is tired of living as a fugitive in a state in which he must renounce his priesthood and marry, or be shot. However, he is constrained by a request for his spiritual and medical services on behalf of a woman he knows will not really need him. Nonetheless, he feels destined to go to her aid. He thus misses the boat from Tabasco. As ironic consequence, we later discover, he escapes capture on the boat.

Young Carol Fellows hides the priest in her barn. Meanwhile the lieutenant and his Red Shirts, as Garrido Canabal—rationalist and puritannical dictator of Tabasco—called them, search for him on her premises. Escaping detection, the priest moves further inland to Concepcion. From there he journeys to the village where his daughter, Brigida, and her mother, Maria, live. Expecting hospitality, the priest does not find it at the village; the people protect him but fear reprisal by the lieutenant. This fanatic has already killed a hostage in Concepcion when they would not tell of the priest's whereabouts, and he plans the same procedure everywhere the priest has been sheltered.

The priest's brief visit with his daughter after six years causes him considerable pain. He loves her terribly, but Brigida rejects him, cares nothing for his Christian values, and suffers because the other children know she is a priest's daughter. The priest is moved to a sacrificial vow, in which he offers his own soul in return for the child's salvation. After he does so, Brigida seems to cease struggling and listens attentively to him for the first time. Though the priest still worries about her, it is possible to assume that his prayer for his daughter is answered. At any rate, this last scene in which we see Brigida is a hopeful one. It is difficult for me to understand why critics miss this hope and see Brigida as lost and the priest as despairing over his certitude that she is lost.

The priest says Mass for the people in the early morning while the lieutenant and his Red Shirts approach from Concepcion. His sermon, interestingly enough, is about heaven, the very topic the lieutenant accuses the Church of using as an opiate. Ironically, the priest and the lieutenant see heaven in similar terms. The priest preaches a heaven in an afterlife that has no unjust laws, no taxes, no hunger, no soldiers. The lieutenant's heaven has the same features, though he expects to see them realized in this life.

As the Red Shirts arrive, the priest hurriedly concludes the Mass. The people anger the lieutenant by not identifying the priest, and he takes young Miguel as hostage. Offering himself as a hostage without identifying himself, the priest is rejected as too old and useless. Still, even Miguel's mother will not betray the priest. When the Red Shirts leave, the priest upbraids the people for their excessive loyalty. He cannot give himself away because that would be to betray a trust God has given him, but they can certainly identify him.

Enroute to the village of Carmen, the priest encounters a mestizo. This man recognizes him and tries to betray him for a reward, but the priest eludes him. Later in Carmen he is arrested for carrying brandy and spends the evening in prison. He identifies himself to his cell mates and is relieved now that he can finally cease running. Still they protect him, and he is released the next morning. The lieutenant himself actually releases him, thinks he looks familiar, but sends him on his way with a gift of money, "the price of a Mass," the priest thinks to himself.

The priest escapes over the mountains and into Chiapas, a state offering relative freedom from persecution. Nevertheless, on his way to Las Casas and a peaceful life, he again meets the mestizo, who wants to return him to Tabasco though he pretends a dying Yankee gangster has requested his services. The priest recognizes the attempt for what it is worth but goes to certain capture thinking the American might just need him.

At long last the lieutenant captures his prey, though he chafes under the knowledge that he has executed men in place of a priest he has had in his grasp but could not recognize. He returns the priest to prison and to death though the priest's genuine humility impresses him in a way the churchmen of his youth had not. The lieutenant even attempts to get the apostate Padre Jose to hear the priest's confession, but Jose and his wife suspect it may be a means of incriminating him. Since Jose will not come, the lieutenant brings the priest a bottle of brandy to help him through his final night.

The priest is executed in the morning, and the lieutenant is rid of the last priest, he believes, but that very night another priest makes his way to the house of Luis.

Among the novel's themes, one of the strongest is the positive value of suffering. In the sermon scene, already mentioned, we find perhaps the most explicit reference to this paradoxical Christian notion:

> "One of the Fathers has told us that joy always depends on pain. Pain is part of joy. We are hungry and then think how we enjoy our food at last. We are thirsty . . ." He stopped suddenly, with his eyes glancing away into the shadows, expecting the cruel laugh that did not come. He said, "We deny ourselves so that we can enjoy. You have heard of rich men in the north who eat salted foods, so that they can be thirsty—for what they call the cocktail. Before the marriage, too, there is the long betrothal . . ." Again he stopped. He felt his own unworthiness like a weight at the back of the tongue. There was a smell of hot wax from where a candle dropped in the nocturnal heat; people shifted on the hard floor in the shadows. The smell of unwashed human beings warred with the wax. He cried out stubbornly in a voice of authority, "That is why I tell you that heaven is here: this is a part of heaven just as pain is a part of pleasure." He said,

" Pray that you will suffer more and more. Never get tired of suffering. The police watching you, the soldiers gathering taxes, the beating you always get from the jefe because you are too poor to pay, smallpox and fever, hunger . . . that is all part of heaven—the preparation. Perhaps without them, who can tell, you wouldn't enjoy heaven so much. Heaven would not be so complete. And heaven, What is heaven?" Literary phrases from what seemed now to be another life altogether—the the strict quiet life of the seminary—became confused on his tongue: the names of precious stones: Jerusalem the Golden. But these people had never seen gold. He went rather stumbling on "Heaven is where there is no jefe, no unjust laws, no taxes, no soldiers and no hunger. Your children do not die in heaven."

I have quoted at length because the sermon's beauty and effect grow as the priest struggles increasingly to show the place of suffering.

Heaven is here because pain is a part of joy, a preparation for joy. Suffering has made this priest grow, though his humility would prevent his even entertaining that thought. Yet the story witnesses to that growth from his parish days, an idle time spent with Altar-Rosary societies, to his real commitment to what he sees as God's will, whatever the personal cost. He longs to cease the struggle, would prefer instant martyrdom to continuous martyrdom, yet he will not give himself up. God's will must manifest itself in a less selfish way.

Moreover, though we are told "the good things of life beckoned to him too early," we find they beckoned to him late as well. He almost returns to the pastoral stance of his early days when he escapes and is given sanctuary by the German Lutheran Lehrs. Insidious as luxury is, the priest nearly succumbs to its lures here. Only a conscious effort allows him to escape a life-style like that of his pampered past.

Reinforcing the theme of suffering's value is the Christ-Judas symbolism of the novel. The priest rides to Carmen on a mule in a manner reminiscent of Christ's Palm-Sunday entrance into Jerusalem. He is led by a mestizo who, recognizing him, wishes to turn him over to the Red Shirts and collect a reward. Although the priest sees through the mestizo's pretended piety and escapes, he later allows the mestizo to lead him to capture and death when not to do so would mean not to come to the spiritual aid of the dying Yankee. His time has now come, and the reader recalls the parallel in John's gospel when Christ fled across the Jordan to avoid being stoned, yet shortly thereafter voluntarily went up to Jerusalem and capture. The Christ-Judas parallels are many and they implicitly lend to the priest biblical suggestions of the suffering Lamb of God and the concomitant redemptive value.

An even more effective means of dramatizing the theme that suffering is a positive force lies in the effective juxtaposition of a fictionalized martyrdom and a real martyrdom. In several scenes of the novel, a pious Catholic mother reads to her children from a saccharine martyrology of a young saint named Juan:

> "Young Juan," the mother read, "from his earliest years was noted for his humility and piety. Other boys might be rough and revengeful; young Juan followed the precept of Our Lord and turned the other cheek. One day his father thought that he had told a lie and beat him. Later he learnt that his son had told the truth, and he apologised to Juan. But Juan said to him, 'Dear father, just as our Father in heaven has the right to chastise when he pleases . . .'"
> The boy rubbed his face impatiently against the whitewash and the mild voice droned on. The two little girls sat with beady intense eyes, drinking in the sweet piety.
> "We must not think that young Juan did not laugh and play like other children, though there were times when he would creep away with a holy picture-book to his father's cow house from the circle of his merry playmates."
> The boy squashed a beetle with his bare foot and thought gloomily that after all everything had an end—someday they would reach the last chapter and young Juan would die against a wall shouting, "Viva el Christo Rey."

So unreal does the wôman's young son, Luis, find the tale that he objects aloud and is sent to his room. Even the apostate priest, Padre Jose, is seen as a more genuine martyr, one who suffers daily the pangs of conscience and the taunts of children. In need of a hero figure, then, Luis turns to the lieutenant, who hunts the priest. However, when he witnesses the execution of the priest, a less edifying but more genuine martyr than the fictionalized Juan, a priest who has spent this last night with brandy and self-recrimination, and who staggers to his death without shouting, "Viva el Christo Rey," young Luis has found his hero. He spits at the lieutenant's gun in revulsion.

The whole story is essentially framed by the two incidents involving Luis, and a flesh and blood man's coping with suffering and death has an effective foil in the Juan of the martyrology who welcomes suffering as though he were donning an alb and stole.

The second major theme of the novel is the presence of the supernatural in our world. This theme is perhaps most explicitly revealed in the conversations between the priest and the lieutenant after the former is captured:

> "That's another difference between us. It's no good your working for your end unless you're a good man yourself. And there won't always be good men in your party. Then you'll have all the old starvation, beating, get-rich- anyhow. But it doesn't matter so much my being a coward— and all the rest. I can put God into a man's mouth just the same—and I can give him God's pardon. It wouldn't make any difference to that if every priest in the Church was like me."

The priest points to the fact that the Church's sacraments work, if I may use the technical and somewhat untranslatable theological expressions, *ex opere operato* and not *ex opere operantis*. In other words, the grace conferred on one who receives the sacraments does not depend upon the worthiness of the minister. It depends on the strength of the sacrament itself (*ex opere operato*). The lieutenant's program depends entirely upon a succession of ministers, i.e. administrators, as worthy as himself. Thus his program works *ex opere operantis*, or on the strength only of the one who implements it.

Somewhat later in their discussion, the lieutenant and the priest turn to the subject of the miraculous:

> "I can't think how a man like you can believe in those things. The Indians, yes. Why, the first time they see an electric light they think it's a miracle."
> "And I dare say the first time you saw a man raised from the dead you might think so too." He giggled unconvincingly behind the smiling mask. "Oh, it's funny, isn't it? It isn't a case of miracles not happening—it's just a case of people calling them something else. Can't you see the doctors round the dead man? He isn't breathing anymore, his pulse has stopped, his heart's not beating: he's dead. Then somebody gives him back his life, and they all—what's the expression?—reserve their opinion. They won't say it's a miracle, because that's a word they don't like.

> Then it happens again and again perhaps—because God's about on earth—and they say: these aren't miracles, it is simply that we have enlarged our conception of what life is. Now we know you can be alive without pulse, breath, heartbeats. And they invent a new word to describe that state of life, and they say science has disproved a miracle." He giggled again. "You can't get round them."

The same theme is implicit throughout the novel. Several characters who come in contact with this humble priest seem to have their lives touched by God in some small but significant way. Luis, as we have seen, moves from a rejection of Christian martyrs to an admiration of this priest-martyr and a rejection of the revolutionary heroes. Coral Fellows turns from atheism to a questioning of God's existence; and an English dentist, Tench, who entertains the priest fugitive in the novel's opening scene, is moved to write his estranged wife for the first time in twenty years. Likewise Brigida, discussed above, seems to show some improvement during her last few moments with her father.

The novel never forces a supernatural explanation for any of these phenomena, and the reader is able to view them as accidents much as the doctor can explain the resuscitation of a dead man as a natural occurrence. Thus the author saves himself an embarrassment here that he will feel in *The End of the Affair* where certain phenomena could not in the original version be explained as natural. Nevertheless, the novel impresses the receptive reader by its supposition that grace and even the miraculous are operative in our world.

The novel's point-of-view serves its themes very well. For most of the story, the priest is the focus of vision. Since he is a humble man, he makes much of his failings and little of his virtues. Thus the reader compensates for the way this man underrates himself. An omniscient narrator, not giving a self-effacing viewpoint, would have run the risk of displeasing the reader with hagiographic argument more like that Luis' mother reads to him. A first-person narration would have centered our attention more on those whom the priest encountered than on the priest himself. In the scenes where the focus shifts from the priest, it centers almost always on the lieutenant, who is a secular priest himself. "There was something of a priest in his intent observant walk— a theologian going back over the errors of the past to destroy them again." An ascetic who feels no sympathy for the weaknesses of the flesh, the lieutenant is the perfect antagonist for the priest. By giving him virtues the priest does not possess and few moral weaknesses, the story encourages our sympathy for the lieutenant. Thus, the eventual confrontation between the two men is not weighted unfairly for the priest however much we sense where the author's final sympathies lie.

The setting's appropriateness as a kind of metaphor for the spiritual state of Mexico is apparent. From the opening scene on we are made to feel the blazing sun in the bleached dust, the vultures looking after the carrion on one side of the town square and the sharks in the river on the other; and between them Mr. Tench is backed up in his work on decayed teeth. The only sense of life and purpose is the lieutenant's fanatical search for the one remaining priest and the priest's ever diminishing efforts to escape and to serve the people.

Later, during the scene in the prison cell, the reader feels again the appropriateness of the scene as a metaphor for the world. We smell the urine and vomitus, hear the sex act as well as the religious hypocrisies, feel the intense heat and the mosquitoes, "This place was very like the world: overcrowded with lust and crime and unhappy love, it stank to heaven, but he realized that after all it was possible to find peace there, when you knew for certain that the time was short."

The theme of suffering is again reinforced by this setting. In this foul cell, the priest senses the common bond between all suffering men, and affection prevails over nausea. "Again he was touched by an extraordinary affection. He was just one criminal among a herd of criminals . . . He had a sense of companionship which he never experienced in the old days when pious people came kissing his black cotton glove."

Near the novel's end, while the priest is being executed, Mr. Tench tries to remove the teeth of the police jefe as he himself is doubled with indigestion. Throughout the reader is made to feel the aridity and sickness of this society, as well as its possibilities for redemption.

I mentioned at this chapter's beginning that the novel's success comes from rendering its allegory in realistic terms, from refusing to orchestrate an unequal battle between the powers of God and the powers of Mammon. This integrity is seen more clearly when one contrasts the novel with its movie version.[1] In John Ford's 1947 film, the viewer is given one hero, the priest, played by Henry Fonda. Renamed *The Fugitive*, the film offers a corrupt lieutenant, played by Pedro Armendariz, makes him, rather than the priest, father of Brigida, has the priest turn down even a glass of brandy on going to his execution, and gives a greater role to the American gangster, played by Ward Bond. Ford thought highly of his film and might have been correct in assuming the American audience of the '40s would not have accepted the priest as Greene created him nor the lieutenant as equal adversary.

The reaction to the 1961 television version seems to corroborate Ford's opinion. When CBS presented the show, with an impressive cast including Lawrence Olivier as the priest, George C. Scott as the lieutenant, and Julie Harris as Maria, it received letters of outrage at its depiction of a whisky priest and his illegitimate daughter.

Greene's novel, then, did not pandar to our traditional expectations regarding a hero nor to our desire for a clear distinction between good and evil. Though Greene had hated Mexico as much as he had loved Africa, had detested its banishment of God for the dusty rationalism of Herbert Spencer, he did not allow his personal response to militate against his writer's judgment. He had encountered several possible models for his priest but none for such a lieutenant. Still he isolated the more admirable qualities of Garrido Canabal and Saturnino Cedillo and gave the strengths of these two dictators to his lieutenant, thereby creating the worthy antagonist for his priest and the complex novel that emerges.

The themes of suffering, of the divided self (the priest's), of lost childhood (the lieutenant's), and of the presence of the supernatural are familiar ones. Yet he had never found the vehicle for so many of his major themes before, and perhaps never would again.

## Chapter Six

# *THE MINISTRY OF FEAR* (1943)

*The Ministry of Fear* is set in wartime London, and in his introduction to the Collected Edition, Greene remarks that "the author of 'The Napoleon of Notting Hill' would have loved those days." What Greene suggests G. K. Chesterton would have loved is that people did not wander far from their own villages in wartime London. An attachment for one's village or city-state was of course dear to the medievalist Chesterton. Still there are other elements in this novel that are reminiscent of G.K.C.'s novel: the preference for nationalism to the supranationalism of Tolstoy or Shaw, one man's romantic struggle against a powerful and insidious enemy, a real awareness of the forces of evil in the world, and the need of the individual to preserve spiritual values in a society that has lost them.

*The Ministry of Fear* is the first of what Greene used to call his "entertainments" that we have considered. Essentially in such works plot dominates, as in a good mystery thriller. Nevertheless, the reader can soon understand why Greene dropped his distinction between novels and entertainments. Arthur Rowe is a much more complex character than the standard protagonist of a mystery thriller or crime novel. Moreover, the thematic element assumes a considerably greater role than it does in the thriller, a role more akin to that played by the political, social, or religious themes in Greene's other novels. Not only are the Chestertonian virtues contended for by Greene's protagonist, but the case for pity's being a cruel, destructive force is as vehemently argued here as in Greene's next novel, *The Heart of the Matter*.

*The Ministry of Fear* opens in an Edenic garden as Arthur Rowe attends a fête that "called him like innocence: it was entangled in childhood, with vicarage gardens and girls in white summer frocks and the smell of herbaceous borders and security." At the fête he wins a cake intended for a Nazi spy, a cake containing a microfilm of which Rowe is unaware, but which results in attempts on his life by poison, by bomb, then worse still on his mind by Dr. Forester, a quack in the employ of the Nazis. Along the way Rowe falls in love with Anna Hilfe, sister of the story's most insidious Nazi, and look-alike for his own dead wife. Rowe had poisoned his wife with hyoscine in an act of euthanasia for which he lives in perpetual guilt.

After suffering amnesia from an explosion intended to kill him, Rowe is incarcerated in Dr. Forester's sanatorium for three months. Eventually he escapes from this surrealistic setting when newspapers imprudently supplied by Forester's assistant, Johns, return part of his memory. He makes his way to Scotland Yard and helps Inspector Prentice pursue the missing microfilm and the espionage ring. The police in turn help him by jogging his memory. The espionage ring, or ministry of fear, is gradually tracked down, and Rowe secures the microfilm from Willi Hilfe. However, pity takes hold of him again, and he returns Hilfe's gun, allowing him to kill himself before capture. At the story's end, Anna and Rowe are united and he seeks a kind of atonement in having to pretend permanently to Anna that he remembers nothing about having killed his wife and suffers no guilt thereby.

The novel's plot has the labyrinthine complexity common to so many of Greene's entertainments and to the best detective stories. Rowe's prize cake brings violence, fear, and mystery into his life for reasons he cannot understand and that he cannot make clear to anyone whose aid he enlists.

Only in bits and pieces does Rowe, or the reader, receive the clues that help him understand. Not until mid-story, when he is recovering from amnesia in the sanatorium, does Rowe learn of a German ministry of fear, which gets a hold on people and spreads an atmosphere of distrust and intimidation. Here too he and the reader learn that a microfilm was stolen from the Ministry of Home Security, and we are thus able to understand that the microfilm was hidden in the cake. Later in the story, Rowe learns that a murder for which he believed he was being sought never occurred, that it was a hoax meant to discourage his pursuit of the spies and drive him underground. He learns also that a bomb intended to destroy him destroyed only his memory, and he is thus kept in Forester's sanatorium. Little by little Rowe and the reader come to understand the nightmarish world into which he was hurled when in an idyllic garden scene he took a cake not intended for him.

The story is told with a mastery that keeps its most involved twistings and turnings under control. Never does one scene give us so much of this fantastic story that we find ourselves incredulous or not driven on for more. In fact, only one item strains credibility at all. The item is Willi Hilfe's death. Why does he kill himself instead of Rowe with the gun Rowe rashly returns? Hilfe tells Rowe it is because he fears capture and torture and because he wishes Rowe to suffer from the knowledge he has returned to him, that Rowe killed his wife. The reason does not quite convince. Nevertheless, the manner of Hilfe's end is not essential to the story, and the criticism of the handling of it is minor. So many implausible occurrences are made plausible in this exciting tale that Paramount Studios chose not to be so ambitious as the author. They eliminated the essential and well-written sanatorium section from the film. As a result, the gifted director, Fritz Lang, created an effective opening to a film that thereafter lost its complexity and reverted to wartime spy melodrama.[1]

How does Greene convey values in so complex and fast-moving a tale without obtruding or losing credibility? The wartime defense of nationalism occurs implicitly as Rowe reads Dr. Forester's books, particularly his copy of Tolstoy's *What I Believe*. Forester has made pencil marks next to certain sections, then erased those marks, and Rowe dwells on passages a man has marked but believes he must erase. Tolstoy had written:

> What seemed to me good and lofty—love of fatherhood, of one's own people—became to me repulsive and pitiable. What seemed to me bad and shameful—rejection of fatherhood and cosmopolitanism—now appeared to me on the contrary good and noble.

Rowe's disdain for supranationalism or cosmopolitanism and for all such transcendent idealism is then captured in his reflection on the passage, "Idealism had ended up with a bullet in the stomach at the foot of the stairs [the murder of Forester by Johns]; the idealist had been caught out in treachery and murder."

The intellectual arrogance of the pan-Europeans and supranationalists is evident in all the Fifth Columnists. When the repulsive cripple, Poole, for whom the cake was intended, visits Rowe to get the cake or the microfilm back, he criticizes narrow patriotism. Intelligent men like Rowe and himself should be above that. As he harps on intelligence, Rowe thinks, "It was as if intelligence was the password to some small exclusive society."

Rowe is not the Carlylean Poole is, does not, like Poole, read *Heroes and Hero Worship* or the lives of Napoleon and Cromwell. Life is not peopled by grand figures doing battle. As he later listens to the duffer, Rennit, at his detective agency, Rowe thinks:

> You couldn't take such an odd world seriously, and yet all the time, in fact, he took it with a mortal seriousness. The grand names stood permanently like statues in his mind: names like Justice and Retribution, though what they both boiled down to was simply Mr. Rennit, hundreds and hundreds of Mr. Rennits. But of course if you believed in God—and the Devil—the thing wasn't quite so comic. Because the Devil—and God too—had

> always used comic people, futile people, little suburban natures and the maimed and warped to serve his purposes. When God used them you talked emptily of Nobility and when the devil used them of Wickedness, but the material was only dull shabby human mediocrity in either case.

Both Dr. Forester and Arthur Rowe are dull shabby mediocrity. One is transformed into Wickedness and the other into Nobility. It is to suggest this implicitly that Greene uses the epigrams from *The Little Duke* at the head of each chapter. They suggest the parallel between ordinary Arthur Rowe and Richard the Fearless of Charlotte Yonge's medieval romance. Greene's Chestertonian Romantisicm emerges.

The other, more central, thematic issue is pity's destructive power. Pity forces Rowe, against his own inclination, to help a seedy old man carry his valise of books. The books turn out to be a bomb. Pity makes Rowe return Hilfe's gun, and thus keep him from the police, who need his evidence. Pity makes Johns kill his admired employer, Forester, and likewise keep him from the police. And, most central, pity brings Rowe to poison his wife. The reader sees the first three acts of pity as negative because of their consequences. There is no authorial comment. The fourth act is one for which the story might seem at first to enlist sympathy. However, it is clear that Rowe comes to believe it wrong. His wife might have preferred any existence to no existence. And who is to say, Rowe reasons, that it is not himself he pities in eliminating his suffering wife?

Though indirect and unobtrusive, the author's indictment of pity is firm. The reader at first nods agreement with jury and friends who tell Rowe he is guiltless despite poisoning his wife. Then the same reader sees the extent to which Dr. Forester and the Nazis employ euthanasia. Old and infirm can be justifiably eliminated for the good of the state when economy is necessary for the republic at large. Likewise those who interfere with the espionage ring are eliminated, not in vindictiveness but by virtue of a "higher" cause. There is no wholesale murder. Economy, Rowe learns, is the key word. If he need not be killed for the cause, he will be comfortably kept in the sanatorium. Reason prevails. From the first Nazi Rowe meets he learns that intelligence is a kind of password into a small exclusive society. And it is a significant comment on Rowe's own poisoning of his wife that the Nazi tries to kill him with the same poison, hyoscine, when all other means of securing the microfilm fail. The reader is thus made to feel that this intelligent, reasonable, pitying act of euthanasia is too simplistic an answer to a complex question. Human problems deserve much more than the reasonable answers of the Nazis.

The characters in Greene's entertainments are never mere servants of plot. Arthur Rowe suffers from the same pity that will give such complexity to Scobie in Greene's next novel. Pity drives Rowe to kill his wife, and he later feels guilty despite acquittal by jury. However, Rowe develops as Scobie will not. Following incarceration in the sanatorium, Rowe progressively jettisons his former pity. He feels little for the Nazi, Cost, who kills himself to escape Prentice and Rowe. He feels nothing for Dr. Forester and his assistant, Poole, when Johns kills them. When Willi Hilfe returns to Rowe the memory of having killed his wife, the old guilt and pity do not return. He can handle the information. Yet Rowe is not completely cured in this final book, "The Whole Man. " He succumbs once more to pity, as we have seen, when he allows Hilfe to take his own life. In knowing what he should do but in failing to do it, to "put off the old man," Rowe emerges as a complex character. This sentimental, romantic man, who goes to fêtes because they remind him of his youth, who reads only *David Copperfield*, *The Old Curiosity Shop*, and books that he read as a boy, who moves through off-limits parts of the sanatorium like Pathfinder, encounters all the modern forces of evil and strangely enough prevails. Yet he never fully learns what all these wolves in sheep's clothing should have taught him, the destructiveness of pity. Human nature changes slowly, and Rowe's case so aptly demonstrates the point.

This is the first time we have discussed what will become an increasingly common theme in Greene: the destructiveness of a virtue's excess. We will see it again in *The Heart of the Matter,* in *The Human Factor* and elsewhere. However, though the concern only gradually occupies center stage in Greene's works, we can see it *in ovo* from the beginning. Elizabeth kills herself rather than betray Andrews in *The Man Within* and Rose is willing to damn herself with Pinkie in *Brighton Rock*.

The remaining characters of the novel are subordinate to Rowe and do serve primarily to advance the plot. Still several come alive for the brief moments of Rowe's story they are to share. Willi Hilfe's romantic Nazism makes him a convincingly deceptive force of evil. Dr. Forester rises above the type of Nazi villain because he keeps a reasonable and humane sanatorium. Johns continually calls him the "great man," reminding us of another complex "great man," Kurtz of *Heart of Darkness*. His evil too comes from wrong-headedness, from unjustifiable rationalization and not from ill will.

Anna Hilfe, it is true, is the small, feminine, almost androgynous female of so many Greene novels. He seldom is as successful with women as with men in his early novels. However, Prentice, the inspector who deals with the off-beat, psychologically complex cases is somewhat more than another policeman. He is himself off-beat and humane, but unpitying, and aggressive with criminals. In several ways he is Rowe's complement. In the final analysis, however, all these characters occupy a minor role in the story and exist primarily for the plot. Only Rowe seems larger and more important than plot, and it is he who makes the novel more than an entertainment.

## Chapter Seven

# *THE HEART OF THE MATTER* (1948)

In this the third of his religious novels, Greene writes the genuine tragedy that he came close to writing in many of his other novels. His protagonist, Major Scobie, is a virtuous man whose *hamartia*, or tragic flaw, lies in the excess of pity he possesses. Pity is not itself a vice but a virtue. Nonetheless, as Arthur Rowe discovered in *The Ministry of Fear*, its excess will trap and betray us. Rowe had come to see that "it wasn't only evil men who did these things. Courage smashes a cathedral, endurance lets a city starve, pity kills . . . we are trapped and betrayed by our virtues."

In Scobie, as in Rowe, pity exceeds all bounds and becomes as vicious as does Macbeth's ambition. Scobie's pity wrecks a marriage he tries to save, ruins a lover he had hoped to help, kills his closest friend—his "boy" Ali, and brings about the moral corruption of Scobie's character, a character earlier compared to that of Aristides the Just by one person and to that of the Old Testament's Daniel by another. Before he finally destroys his life, Scobie has already destroyed his character by adultery, smuggling, treason, lies, sacrilege, and murder.

Scobie is a fifty-year-old deputy police commissioner in Sierra Leone during World War II. He and his wife Louise had earlier lost their young daughter, Catherine, and thus Louise has no one here in West Africa but her husband. Snobbery and her bookish tastes make "literary Louise" an object of scorn for other colonials. However, since pathetic creatures bring out in Scobie the only love he seems able to experience, he has promised God in a private vow to sacrifice his own peace to make Louise happy. He is not able to do that, though for a long while he can see her through her depressed moods. He even jeopardizes his reputation and position by borrowing £200 from the Syrian smuggler, Yusef, in order to send Louise, at her own insistence, to South Africa. Still, he and Louise might have struggled through the problem of day-to-day living had not a greater object of pity entered on the scene.

While Louise is away, a boat is torpedoed, and among the survivors is nineteen-year-old Helen Rolt. Helen's husband of one month has been killed, and Scobie's first sight of the scrawny, unattractive young girl is as she is carried on a stretcher, clutching a stamp collection book. Scobie is moved, and because she desperately needs this kind and attentive man, an affair Scobie neither expected nor wanted develops.

Louise comes home after seven months because she has been told about Scobie's deception. However, she never broaches the matter directly to him. Instead she prods him to come to Mass and to receive Communion with her, arguing that she worries he has not been a good Catholic while she was away. Since Scobie cannot promise a confessor that he will not see Helen again because he clearly intends to, he is refused absolution and is forced in desperation to take Communion sacrilegeously, while in the state of sin. He now begins to despair and contemplates suicide. No one will need him, no one will make demands upon him and no one will be hurt by him once he is dead. As a Catholic, he realizes suicide is the unforgiveable sin, but there are always exceptions, "Christ had not been murdered—you couldn't murder God: Christ had killed himself." Scobie pretends to have the symptoms of angina, is given evipan, pretends to take one each day, but saves them up to administer a fatal dose. Take the dose he does, and the novel ends with three short scenes in which Louise and Wilson, a government man sent to spy on Scobie and others and who in the process falls in love with Louise, discuss Scobie's death. With his detective's eye, Wilson notices that Scobie's diary entries about the evipan have not been made over a period of time. They were merely made to seem so entered in order to avoid the suspicion of suicide. With that heinous crime revealed, Louise loses what little respect for her husband she had left. In the second scene, Helen, who has been drinking heavily since Scobie's death, gives herself to a worthless soldier without any feeling in the matter. Finally, Louise and Father Rolt discuss Scobie and, at her insistence that the Church teaches he has cut himself off from mercy, Father Rolt angrily responds that "the Church knows all the rules. But it doesn't know what goes on in a single human heart."

The author intended Scobie's pity as an act of "almost monstrous pride," and Scobie himself seems to recognize the pride, "Make me put my own soul first. Give me trust in your mercy to the one I abandon." But Scobie cannot trust God to take up the slack he leaves, and so he must sacrifice his life so that "the others [might]get some happiness."

The new Collected Edition of the novel restores to the story an early scene between Wilson and Louise Scobie. Greene had written it for the original, then withdrawn it since he believed that, told as it was from Wilson's point of view, it broke Scobie's point of view prematurely. With its return, Louise is seen in a more sympathetic light, and we do not necessarily see Scobie as one hunted to his death by Louise. Though the reader is still tempted to like Scobie and in large part to exonerate him, he likely will not read the present text without seeing Scobie's excess of pity for what it is. That pity is borne in upon us time and again, and only to the extent that we are unaccustomed to view pity as anything but a virtue can we fail to be appalled by the otherwise attractive Scobie, "If one knew, he wondered, the facts, would one have to feel pity even for the planets? if one reached what they called the heart of the matter?"

*The Heart of the Matter*, then, resumes the indictment of pity that earlier *The Ministry of Fear* had made. There the criticism of pity ran: once commit an intrinsically wrong act out of pity and you will eventually be able to commit an intrinsically wrong act out of economy. Arthur Rowe, we saw, had killed his wife in an act of euthanasia and society told him he was guiltless. But the Nazis killed the old and infirm for reasons of economy and the good of the state at large. In *The Heart of the Matter*, the case may be made more subtly, but Scobie acts out of the same implicit arrogance as do the Nazis. He too plays God. We may find him justified when he first pities a Portugese ship's captain who, against the law, is smuggling a letter to his daughter, but the same virtue that leads Scobie to break the rules here leads eventually to his playing Christ in offering himself as a sacrificial victim for the two women.

The novel's three final, anti-climactic scenes serve effectively to reduce the grandeur of his act and show the utter waste his suicide was and the fearful pride contained in his act. It is not that the final scenes make Scobie seem a lesser person. On the contrary, his wife and Helen are made to appear more unworthy of him: Louise with her unkind judgments, judgments about Scobie's taking money from Yusef when that very money was borrowed to send her to South Africa as she wanted; and Helen giving her body to Bagster immediately after Scobie's death. Nonetheless, the very criticism of these women makes Scobie's suicide more meaningless and shows up still more effectively the arrogance of his action.

If the structuring of the novel to provide the three anti-climactic episodes and if the change in point-of-view to let us see Louise in a better light both help the author's theme, the structure and point-of-view in general are equally well chosen. Greene has an orderly arrangement of three parts: Book One depicting the relationship between Scobie and Louise; Book Two that between Scobie and Helen; and Book Three bringing all the characters together. This arrangement not only provides time to have the reader know and sympathize with each of Scobie's women, thus building a dilemma with horns of equal proportion, but it builds suspense as we wait for the *dramatis personae* to come together and force Scobie to a resolution.

The point-of-view is a remnant of an earlier tale Greene had intended to tell: a "crime story" in which the readers know the criminal but in which the detective is unknown. Enough of that tale remains in the narrator's focus on Scobie's moral demise and the gradual revelation of Wilson's function. Scobie in fact is the last to understand Wilson's identity. The effect of this focus is that we see Scobie's spiritual disintegration from within. Had we seen this process from a distance, the effect clearly would have been to diminish the importance of Scobie's problem. Tragedy would not have been possible.

There are several other devices that serve to dramatize the theme of this novel. One is a symbol that the author used thirteen years earlier in *England Made Me*, the Tristram and Iseult motif. Here Wilson sees himself as Tristram, who has drunk the love potion forever attaching him to Louise (Iseult) and necessitating the struggle with her husband, Scobie (Mark). Actually the absurd romanticism of Wilson, whose feelings are not reciprocated by Louise, is a parody of the real tragic triangle, that between Scobie, Louise, and Helen; and the love potion that attaches Scobie tragically to both women is, of course, the pity that he has drunk of too deeply.

Another device that serves to dramatize the theme is the use of a minor character as a foil for Scobie. The Syrian trader, Yusef, is the best-realized character in the novel after Scobie. From the moment we meet this man who is genuinely attached to Scobie, we know that he is Scobie's opposite. He lacks pity entirely. Scobie stops to give him a lift when his car has broken down. When Yusef gratefully climbs in, Scobie suggests Yusef's boy get in back, but Yusef makes the boy remain with the car since "he will mind the car if he knows it is the only way he can get to bed."

Later, when Scobie has lost trust in his own boy, Ali, he talks to Yusef about him. Yusef does not agonize or sentimentalize. He does not, as does Scobie, choose to render the boy harmless while vacillating about whether he wants to take the means to his end. Yusef has the boy seized and he is killed. Even if Yusef did not order that Ali be killed, he cares little that he has been. Scobie is safe. Scobie pretends to himself that he is above such methods. Yusef's straightforwardness shows Scobie's rationalization for what it is.

Still another device used effectively is setting. The novel opens with Wilson on the balcony of the Bedford Hotel, looking out over the sloping tin roofs to the sea as a vulture noisily alights on the corrugated iron roof above him. We see the quay, the ships, the prostitutes fighting for the sailors and hear the vulture shifting once again as Scobie comes into view. It is a place of primitive passion that the white man likes to think he stands above.

Later we see this African setting through the eyes of Scobie:

Why, he wondered, swerving the car to avoid a

> pye dog, do I love this place so much? Is it because here human nature hasn't had time to disguise itself? Nobody here could ever talk about a heaven on earth. Heaven remained rigidly in its proper place on the other side of death, and on this side flourished the injustices, the cruelties, the meanness that elsewhere people so cleverly hushed up. Here you could love human beings nearly as God loved them, knowing the worst: you didn't love a pose, a pretty dress, a sentiment artfully assumed.

Not only can sin and corruption not disguise itself, virtue cannot either. Scobie's pity for both his wife and for Helen is seen by both women for what it is. Thus his pretense at love is utterly wasted. He somehow imagines the setting accords him a privilege not accorded others.

Greene had trouble writing this novel. His hand, he tells us, had grown rusty from disuse and from misuse in writing wartime telegrams and reports. Still the prose of his final product does not betray his difficulties.

With his customary skill, he can telescope a whole pattern of customs into one brief scene:

> "Your landlady, " Scobie told the girl sharply, "she says you make plenty trouble: too many lodgers, too many lamps." [She had been accused of stealing a lamp and her landlady had pulled down the partition in her house and taken her chest.]
> "No sir. No lamp palaver."
> "Mammy palaver, eh? You bad girl?"
> "No sir."
> "Why you come here? Why you not call Corporal Laminah in Sharp Town?"
> "He's my landlady's brother, sir."
> "He is, is he? Same father, same mother?"
> "No, sir. Same father. "
> The interview was like a ritual between priest and server. He knew exactly what would happen when one of his men investigated the affair. The landlady would say that she had told her tenant to pull down the partitions and when that failed she had taken action herself. He would turn out not to be the landlady's brother, but some other unspecified relation—probably disreputable. Bribes—which were known respectably as dashes—would pass to and fro, the storm of indignation and anger

> that had sounded so genuine would subside, the partitions would go up again, nobody would hear anymore about the chest, and several policemen would be shilling or two the richer. At the beginning of his service Scobie had flung himself into these investigations."

Perhaps a better instance of the effectiveness of Greene's writing is the skill with which he expresses an insight about scenes that remain with you when you have no idea at the time they will. He is speaking about Wilson's first glimpse of Scobie from the balcony of the Bedford Hotel where he is sipping gin and bitters:

> "Look down there," Harris said, "look at Scobie."
> A vulture flapped and shifted on the iron roof and Wilson looked at Scobie. He looked without interest in obedience to a stranger's direction, and it seemed to him that no particular interest attached to the squat grey-haired man walking up Bond Street. He couldn't tell that this was one of those occasions a man never forgets: a small cicatrice had been made on the memory, a wound that would ache whenever certain things combined—the taste of gin at mid-day, the smell of flowers under a balcony, the clang of corrugated iron, an ugly bird flopping from perch to perch.

Finally, the kind of Christian paradox that lies at the crux of so many of Greene's stories is given adroit expression:

> He would still have made the promise (to send Louise to South Africa) even if he could have foreseen all that would come of it. He had always been half aware too, from the time he made his terrible private vow that she should be happy, how far *this* action might carry him. Despair is the price one pays for setting oneself an impossible aim. It is, one is told, the unforgiveable sin, but it is a sin the corrupt or evil man never practices. He always has hope. He never reaches the freezing-point of knowing absolute failure. Only the man of goodwill carries always in his heart this capacity for damnation.

Greene's style and vision, then, combine with his use of point-of-view, structure, setting, symbol, and literary contrast to produce his one genuine tragedy.

The element of tragedy is lost in the 1953 film version of the book when a generally faithful version turns the suicide into murder. Scobie, played by Trevor Howard, prepares to take his life when a fight breaks out in the street, and he goes to rescue someone being beaten up. He is then killed in the line of duty. As he dies, he says to his servant: "Tell Mrs. Scobie that God made it alright—for her." Thus God has intervened and allowed Scobie time to repent of his original intention. This repentance in place of Greene's ambiguous ending, coupled with Scobie's virtuous response to duty, precludes tragedy.

The casting also confused the theme by having the beautiful and talented Maria Schell play Helen. Ms. Schell's handsome looks and maturity were bound to confuse an audience about Scobie's motivation in the liaison. The pity that was conjured up in him at the sight of a plain nineteen-year-old child gripping her stamp album as she was carried from a shipwreck gives way to the suggestion of genuine sexual attraction and love.[1]

I intend no invidious comparison here between a novel and its film version. Such comparisons always seem unfair. What I do intend is merely to help see the novel more clearly by contrast with the film. Allott and Farris have talked about the stylistic severity of *The Heart of the Matter*,[2] meaning that in no novel does Greene depend for his theme so entirely on the unadorned and uninterpreted drama of the human situation. Even *The Power and the Glory* has sections in which the priest and the lieutenant become spokesmen for opposing views of Life. Not so *The Heart of the Matter*. To change, then, one character or one situation is to upset a very delicate balance and create a very different story from the one Greene told, whatever that story's own intrinsic merits.

## Chapter Eight

## *THE END OF THE AFFAIR* (1959)

*The End of the Affair* probably projects its author's "protestant" voice in a "Catholic" society farther than had the previous three religious novels. In *Brighton Rock*, Greene has spoken in behalf of a conscienceless criminal; in *The Power and the Glory* in behalf of a whisky priest; in *The Heart of the Matter* for a suicide. Here the author seems to protest not simply for the sanctity of one who has turned from adultery but perhaps for that sanctity even while she engages in adultery.

Sarah Miles is an adultress but one whose love of her lover turns ultimately into a love of her God. Nonetheless, I do not believe Greene writes here of a sinner turned saint, one who turns away from a moral law and then turns back to it. Rather, he makes the reader understand and love the woman even *while* she is cuckolding her husband, much the same as he makes his reader love Maurice Castle even as Castle betrays his country in *The Human Factor*. Furthermore, Sarah never acknowledges wrong-doing with her lover. Neither does she ultimately leave him through a conviction of sin. Rather she leaves him because of an arbitrary vow offered God for her lover's life.

The plot of *The End of the Affair* is simple though its structure is complex. Maurice Bendrix, a novelist, wants to study the habits of a certain statesman, Henry Miles, for a new novel, and, while doing so, falls in love with Henry's wife, Sarah. The love affair, which begins in 1939 and ends in 1944, is brought about by Sarah's inability to have a sexual relationship with her gentle but cold husband. As a matter of fact, Sarah and Henry probably have never consummated their marriage. Thus she turns to Bendrix, but insecurity and jealousy, especially on the part of Bendrix, render the affair unsatisfactory, despite the genuine love each feels for the other. We learn later the affair is doomed from the beginning. Sarah has never considered divorcing her husband because she did not wish to follow the path of her mother, who moved from marriage to marriage.

Several vivid love scenes between Sarah and Bendrix are dramatized, but the last time they make love is at the house of Bendrix during a 1944 air raid. While Sarah is still upstairs in the bedroom, Bendrix goes down to check on damage caused by bombs. One hits directly, leaving him apparently dead and buried under rubble. Sarah finds him, as she believes, dead. She runs upstairs, falls on her knees, and in her hysterical state, vows to God that she will give up her sexual relationship with Bendrix if God will give her lover a second chance. Bendrix is indeed returned to her, and her trial begins and continues to her death, two years later. Was Bendrix dead? Was he only apparently dead and her vow rash? How can we tell? Even a miracle can appear to have a natural explanation, and—as the unnamed priest in *The Power and the Glory* contends—will appear to the secular mind only to have a natural explanation.

After two years, Sarah dies of a severe cold not remedied soon enough. Her death is followed by some peculiar happenings through which Greene is bold enough to suggest the miraculous. Perhaps the most remarkable of these miracles is the cure of large strawberry mark on the face of Richard Smythe, a rationalist preacher. Sarah had gone to him to be convinced her belief that God intervened to save Bendrix was silly. However, Smythe failed to convince her, and she ultimately affected him more than he could her. Upon Sarah's death, Smythe took a lock of her hair, and this he believes has effected the cure. Partly because he fears the vulgarity of the pious Press and partly because he fears Sarah's God, Bendrix is offended by Smythe's belief.

Bendrix attributes the apparent miracles to hysteria or to coincidence or to whatever natural phenomenon he can. And he fights the God he claims not to believe in with a jealous vengeance. He convinces Henry to cremate Sarah, thus thwarting efforts by a priest to give Sarah a Catholic burial. She had, the priest tells Henry, been taking instructions to enter the church. Despite the gallant fight, however, at book's end Bendrix seems to be fighting a losing battle against God's love.

The miraculous element seemed heavy fare to a good many critics. Greene himself was self-conscious about it. Thus, in the Collected Edition, he made certain changes, and he comments on these changes in his introduction:

> The incident of the strawberry mark should have had no place in the book; every so-called miracle, like the curing of Parkis's boy, ought to have had a completely natural explanation. The coincidences should have continued over the years, battering the mind of Bendrix, forcing on him a reluctant doubt of his own atheism. The last pages would have remained much as they were written (indeed I very much like the last pages), but I had spurred myself too quickly to the end.

> So it is in this edition I have tried to return nearer
> to my original intention. Smythe's strawberry mark
> has given place to a disease of the skin which might
> have had a nervous origin and be susceptible to faith-
> healing.

Making all the miracles amenable of a natural explanation was a wise change. It suggests the possibility of supernatural intervention without forcing a reader to accept that conclusion.[1]

The structure of the novel is a complex one and serves as an excellent vehicle for Greene's subject matter. Maurice Bendrix writes the story in 1949, reverts to the beginning of the affair in 1939, then brings us up to 1946, returns to 1939, then again brings us up to the date that ended the affair with the air raid in 1944. The time sequence jumps back and forth in this way throughout the novel. The only time involving Sarah for which Bendrix cannot account is the period from the end of the affair in 1944 until he writes now in 1949. That period is finally made known to us and to Bendrix when Parkis, the private detective he hired, uncovers Sarah's journal for the period. Then, as we read the journal, we are disarmed by Sarah's goodness, much as the reader of Browning's *Ring and the Book* is disarmed by Pompilia's goodness when he comes to read her monologue. Not surprisingly, Browning was a favorite of Greene.

When Bendrix has finally read the journal, he extends the chronology of this "record of hate," as he calls it, beyond the point of departure he used when beginning his writing. The chronology grows even more complex. And from this point, Bendrix transfers his hatred, for the most part, from Sarah to the God who has, he thinks, replaced him as lover, and the God in whom he does not believe.

Why so complex a structure? I believe the effect of this time sequence in which past impinges on present and present on past, in which Maurice's account not only switches back and forth in time, but within a given time period alludes to events at another period, is to emphasize the narrator's point that the affair has no real past, present, or future. Sarah (and implicitly her divine lover) is as real to Bendrix now as she was in 1939 or 1944 or 1946. Bendrix agrees with Henry that something he had written in an earlier novel about a house being empty when a loved one had died is not true. Henry is right that the house they now share has not a sense of emptiness without Sarah, but too great a sense of her presence. Thus, in a sense, the title is contradictory of the theme. The affair never ends. And the structure's blurring of the distinction between past and present really helps the reader experience the timelessness of this love affair.

In addition to success with structure in the novel, Greene also succeeds with point-of-view. Since Sarah Miles is the central character in the novel, she poses problems for Greene, the problems any realistic novelist faces in trying not only to make goodness but a certain measure of sanctity credible. Greene succeeds by an effective use of point-of-view. He employs a device used by Andre Gide in *La porte étroite*. Both authors have infatuated narrators tell about a character's saintliness. However, Gide's narrator, Jerome, praises Alissa's Jansenistic asceticism, which the reader comes to realize has wrecked the lives of the three main characters. Thus, her spurious goodness is satirized by Gide through a naive narrator. Greene reverses the approach and has a cynical narrator condemn a genuinely good person, thus forcing the reader to make most of the positive inferences about Sarah. The more Maurice condemns Sarah out of hatred, the more we are forced and, as a matter of fact, are inclined to find the good in Sarah.

This form of indirection also aids Greene in treating the delicate subject of the miraculous. Many readers simply could not accept the miraculous if affirmed explicitly. Greene presents three or four instances of the seemingly miraculous, has them questioned by those involved and ridiculed by his narrator. Greene may intend the miracles to be seen as just that, but he does everything, short of denying his belief in the plausibility of supernatural interference in the natural world, to lead the reader to make up his own mind.

Greene's point of view, his use of the jilted lover to narrate the story was just right. We do come to believe in Sarah. It was, however, the first time he had used such a narrator. In the past, he had seemed to accept Percy Lubbock's critical preference for a Jamesian third-person narrator. Now, Greene tells us, he turned to Dickens, a writer he previously found unappealing, read *Great Expectations* and was won by the apparent ease with which Dickens used the first person. Greene did not find the task nearly so easy, and was tempted, once into the writing, to throw it over. How could he achieve Dickens' extraordinary ability to vary tone with a first-person narrator? Would not Bendrix's hate permeate the entire novel? Mr. Parkis, the private detective, and his boy were Greene's way to introduce two more tones, the humorous and the pathetic.

There is one last consideration, however. In offering us a narrator full of hatred for someone we come to like, how does Greene make us accept him as a lover worthy of Sarah? Through a jealous, vindictive lover, Greene can effectively present Sarah's goodness in an oblique manner, but he runs the risk of alienating the reader from Maurice, of making his narrator seem petty and undeserving of sympathy as he jealously explodes at Sarah or uncivilly insults the Catholic priest. However, we come to see Bendrix's good qualities also in an indirect way and to learn that he is an unsparing judge of himself as well as of others. For example,

Maurice's description of his rudeness to the literary critic interviewing him for a review points up his impoliteness. At the same time, however, it reveals Maurice as a man who will not pandar after success. Most of all, though, the fact that what appears unattractive in Maurice's character has been revealed to us by Maurice himself leads the reader to qualify much of the impression this narrator gives of himself.

This last of the religious novels then demonstrates the "virtue of disloyalty" we saw as early as Greene's first novel and will continue to see to the most recent. Moreover, it sounds a still sharper protestant voice in a Catholic society than do the three previous religious novels because it does not offer simply another sinner turned saint by returning to the confines of Catholic moral law. Sarah is not a reformed Magdalen. Whatever God's reason for holding her to her vow, Sarah kept that vow out of loyalty to Him and to herself and not because of any sense of having betrayed her husband, Henry, with Bendrix.

The first journal entry we read, its last page, shows Sarah craving human love with Bendrix as much as or more than before her vow. Sarah, then, is never "converted." Her life and actions are of a piece, and we are asked to understand not that sinner can turn saint, but that an adultress can love God and be loved by God even while she loves her lover.

## Chapter Nine

# *THE QUIET AMERICAN* (1955)

With *The Quiet American*, Greene left his explicitly religious novels behind and returned to the political novel. *The Quiet American* does not, of course, lack a religious and moral dimension anymore than *The Power and the Glory* lacks a political one. However, from this novel on—with the possible exception of *A Burnt-Out Case*—Greene has laid greater emphasis on politics than on religion.

The novel's theme is the peril of naive engagement in a war, in a political situation, or in life itself that one does not understand and the equal peril of pseudo-sophisticated disengagement from the same. It would be surprising had we not already seen it happen, that critics attribute to the author opinions that belong to his character. American critics talk of Greene's strong anti-Americanism in the novel because his first-person narrator, Fowler, displays such feeling. However, the unbiased reader will note that the author is as hard on his narrator's shortcomings as he is on those of his quiet American, Pyle.

Fowler and Pyle are in many ways complementary. Pyle's innocence destroys lives, but he is engaged. Fowler's disengagement also destroys, and his knowledgeability, which poses as informed concern for the Vietnamese, disguises a lack of real compassion. If Pyle were really evidence of Greene's anti-American sentiment, Fowler would be evidence of his anti-British sentiment. This confusion of author and his character is worth dwelling on a moment before we consider the specifics of this novel because, as we have seen, it has been a recurring problem in discussions of Greene. The confusion was made easier in this novel because Fowler shared many of Greene's own feelings about American involvement in Indochina. It was made easier still because the extent of American involment was not yet known in this country. Thus, even the fine radical critic, Philip Rahv, reviewed Greene's novel for *Commentary* as though it were an offensive political tract, and he identified Fowler's desire to eliminate meddling innocents with Greene's opinions.[1]

Still more explicitly identifying author and character, Robert Gorham Davis identified the novel's thesis as "quite simply America is a crassly materialistic and 'innocent' nation with no understanding of other peoples. When her representatives intervene in other countries' affairs, it causes only suffering. America should leave Asians to work out their own destinies even when this means the victory of Communism."[2]

Professor Davis would have distinguished between persona and novelist, but he knew Greene's writings on the war in Indochina. Since they echoed Fowler's ideas, he saw the character as nothing but a spokesman. Thus Greene was prompted to react:

> I would say the theme of the book was religious as well as political. A good deal of the misunderstanding is due to the apparent ignorance nowadays of a novelist's technique. More people should read Henry James' Prefaces and realize the importance of a point of view. If one uses the first person, the point of view has obviously got to be I, and one must put one's self in I's skin as intensely as possible. It would be absurd however to imagine that the author is Fowler any more than he is the boy gangster in "Brighton Rock," which was also told mainly through one point of view. As Pyle stood for complete engagement, Fowler obviously had to stand for an equally exaggerated viewpoint on the other side. Those who have read my war articles on Indochina will know that I am myself by no means a neutralist. I share certain of Fowler's views, but obviously not all of them—for instance, I don't happen to be an atheist. But even those views I share with Fowler I don't hold with Fowler's passion because I don't happen to have lost a girl to an American![3]

The novel is set in Saigon during the French struggle with the Vietcong and, of course, prior to America's direct involvement in the war. At the story's beginning, the English correspondent, Thomas Fowler, and his Vietnamese mistress, Phuong, learn of the assassination of Alden Pyle. This idealistic young American had come to Vietnam fresh from Harvard, spouting book knowledge about the need for a Third Force in Vietnam. Ostensibly he is in the country to work for the Economic Aid Mission, but in reality he is implementing his theories about a Third Force by giving explosives to the tiny and ineffectual army of General Thé. The only result this aid has is the ugly killing and maiming of children and non-participants. Pyle is nauseated by such scenes but continues to believe them a necessity of war. Fowler tries to offer the advantage of his superior knowledge of the Vietnamese and his own experience of years to the younger man, but Pyle, listening deferentially, rejects both.

The situation is further complicated by the fact that Pyle falls in love with Fowler's young mistress and can offer her marriage, whereas Fowler is tied to a wife who will not divorce him. Though Phuong at first rejects the polite offer of Pyle, she later accepts Pyle when Fowler, having received a letter from his wife rejecting divorce, lies to Phuong about the letter's content, and she discovers the lie.

In the meantime, Fowler discovers through Communist contacts that Pyle is responsible for the explosives and allows Pyle to be set up and murdered, pretty much as Scobie had allowed Ali to be set up in *The Heart of the Matter*. Like Scobie too, he convinces himself that the Communists sincerely want only to talk to Pyle. Although Fowler's "disengagement" brings about Pyle's murder, Fowler, not wanting to believe what he has done, waits for Pyle to return from the set-up. Not knowing his part in the murder, Fowler's mistress returns to him, his wife suddenly agrees to divorce, and Phuong wonders why Fowler remains sad.

Fowler has discovered too late his lack of compassion for Pyle, whom he liked, as he had earlier discovered his lack of compassion for another American, the brash Granger, whom he was convinced he disliked until he found suffering in him, "Was I so different from Pyle? I wondered. Must I too have my foot thrust into the mess of life before I saw the pain?"

The novel has an allegorical level at which the three main characters represent, to some extent, their respective countries. Fowler, emblematic of England or of Europe, approaches Phuong with desire but with skepticism about his ability to keep her. Pyle quixotically romances his Dulcinea in the best courtly love tradition, and Phuong passively accepts whoever is kind to her. Significantly Phuong's name means phoenix, and as such she will rise from whatever ashes her colonial protectors reduce her to. The novel, then, intends its political and love fables to go together. Its failure is that the love story is so much weaker than its political counterpart.

After creating his strongest woman character in the previous novel, Greene now creates one of his weakest. So shadowy is Phuong that one suspects Greene of intending this vagueness for allegorical purposes. We hear the voices and feel the presence of England, France, and the United States, but the Vietnamese voice and presence fades far into the background. Still, if this is Greene's intention, it does not help his love story. Fowler's suffering when Phuong deserts him leaves us cold, and the scene is thus one of the few in the author's canon in which he seems to be overstating rather than understating emotion:

I went into the passage. There was a door opposite

> me marked "Men." I went in and locked the door and,
> sitting with my head against the cold wall, I cried.
> I hadn't cried until now. Even their lavatories were
> air-conditioned, and presently the temperate air
> dried my tears as it dries the spit in your mouth
> and the seed in your body.

The passage is nicely written, but we have never sufficiently believed in Phuong to share the least bit of the anguish.

If Phuong does not ring true, both Fowler and Pyle do. The young American is often so irritatingly real that we want to send him back on the first boat to Boston. Yet he is a good man, one who will probably mature, one in whom we recognize many such university people we have known and, perhaps grudgingly, ourselves. His romanticism, though excessive, is endearing so long as it does not enter the arena of war and politics. His sexual innocence, his apologies to Fowler for falling in love with his girl, his slavish addiction to the political theories of York Harding amuse us. His supplying explosives to General Thé horrifies us. We are forced to agree with Fowler about the dangers of innocence. Still Pyle emerges as a complex character toward whom we feel the same attraction and repulsion that Fowler feels.

With few of the attractions of Pyle, Fowler is harder to love. Perhaps his only virtue is the knowledge that comes from experience. His deceit, cynicism, and selfishness make the Englishman less appealing than the American. Yet this anti-Yankee grows, learns compassion however late, and discovers that disengagement will not do. The book ends with his Pyrrhic victory of winning back Phuong:

> I thought of the first day and Pyle sitting beside me
> at the Continental, with his eye on the soda fountain
> across the way. Everything had gone right with me
> since he had died, but how I wished there existed
> someone to whom I could say that I was sorry.

Greene's first-person narrators often prove hardest on themselves, and perhaps he chose such a narrator here for its greater possibilities of irony and subtlety. A third person focus might have presented so evidently flawed a character as Fowler in too unsympathetic a light. Such a focus seems to function better for a Scobie or the Mexican priest, who have enough virtue to carry the reader's sympathy however critically the narrator presents them. Here the less attractive Fowler can at least present his own case.

Could a secondary reason for the author's choosing this focus have been the desire to avoid charges of anti-Americanism? A narrator is more likely to be associated with his author if he is not a character in the story. We have seen this sort of confusion in discussing *England Made Me*, and we will see it again in later novels. Nonetheless, if Greene intended to avoid such criticism in using Fowler as narrator, he did not succeed.

Whatever the author's reasons for choosing the more difficult point of view, the choice creates a few awkwardnesses as it can so easily with a first-person narrator. When Pyle and Fowler argue over who has more to offer Phuong, Fowler defends the temporary relationship he can offer, "She's no child. She's tougher than you'll ever be. Do you know the kind of polish that doesn't take scratches? That's Phuong. She can survive a dozen of us. She'll get old, that's all. She'll suffer from childbirth and hunger and cold and rheumatism, but she'll never suffer like we do from thoughts, obsessions—she won't scratch, she'll only decay." How can we judge this passage since we cannot see Fowler as others see him? The author is compelled to have the narrator himself indicate he rationalizes, "But even while I made my speech and watched her turn the page . . . I knew I was inventing a character just as much as Pyle was."

In another instance, the narrator cannot allow us to judge the action but must provide his readers with an insight into himself by conjecturing what another's expression signifies. The police inspector, Vigot, has just left, and Fowler remarks: "I thought after he had turned and gone that he had looked at me with compassion, as he might have looked at some prisoner for whose capture he was responsible undergoing his sentence for life." Both passages are deftly written under the circumstances, but the author must employ contrivance that would not be necessary could we get behind Fowler and see him as we see other characters in the story.

Finally, a word ought to be said about structure and symbol. Apart from the allegory already discussed, symbol plays a smaller role here than in earlier Greene novels. The only recurrent symbol is the plastics in which Pyle deals and which turn out to be explosives. The plastic culture of America at its worst has become a common enough phrase to make apparent to the reader what the author sees as Pyle's contribution to the problems of Vietnam.

The structure raises more question. It is almost as complex as that of *The End of the Affair*. Beginning with Pyle's death, the story teases the reader with several brief flashbacks to Pyle's story. Several chapters elapse before we are immersed in that story. Moreover, there are chapters that seem intentionally to confuse us by suggesting at first that we are in the present when we later find we are in the past.

Why such complexity? In the early chapters, suspense is surely one motive for the brief glimpses of Pyle that provide just enough to urge us on. However, as the story gets under way, the mingling of past and present can only be intended to make us feel the past as part of the present. Pyle, Fowler, Phuong and what they represent—American idealism and naive innocence, European skepticism, Vietnamese passivity— are not a thing of the past anymore than Pyle's relationship to Phuong and to himself is something Fowler can cease to live with. The structure is effective in conveying this sense, not of course on a conscious level but on a subconscious one. Had the story observed a strict chronology, we would have moved through an experience clearly terminated in Pyle's death. As it is, we cannot remove Pyle and all that he represents from the present.

The novel was transferred to the screen in 1957 by Joseph Manckiewicz, a director-producer who has had several notable successes. He failed in the adaptation of this novel, however, and the changes the film makes throw into relief the strengths of the novel. Gone is the complexity and balance in the characters of Pyle, played by Audie Murphy, and Fowler, played by Michael Redgrave. In its place, the film offers a more unsympathetic Fowler, who in fact causes Pyle's death not from concern over Pyle's naive destructiveness, but solely from jealousy. The novel had allowed for mixed motives, but uppermost in Fowler's mind was Pyle's destructiveness. The movie opted not for ambiguity, but for the simplicity of jealousy. Gone too is the political justification for Fowler's killing Pyle. In a final scene, the detective, Vigot, tells Fowler that Pyle had never been involved with explosives!

Perhaps because American sentiment about Vietnam had not yet turned around, Manckiewicz transformed Pyle into a complete innocent and Fowler into a heavy. The film then ends with the same lack of subtlety. Manckiewicz was not satisfied to leave Fowler with Phuong and guilt ("I wished there existed someone to whom I could say I was sorry.") Rather, at the film's end, Phuong rejects Fowler and chooses to work as a paid escort.

The strength of the novel, then, lies not in what opinion it offers about the Vietnam war or about Americans but in the effectively complex way in which it dramatizes two equally limited views of life. Its strength lies too in the new and convincing dress given to an old obsession: betrayal. Moreover, the novel signals another theme, implicit in earlier novels, that will come to dominate Greene's more recent novels: the need for engagement.

## Chapter Ten

## *OUR MAN IN HAVANA* (1958)

*Our Man in Havana* is the second "entertainment" we will consider, and in one way it represents a substantial change in Greene's method. A rollicking humor began to appear in the *jeu d'esprit*, *Loser Takes All* (1955) and now emerges fully in the present novel. Fortunately, perhaps, the material that suggested this story to Greene had been germinating for some fifteen years since he had worked for the Secret Intelligence Service in Lisbon. Without this lapse of time, the novel's tone might have been far different.

In Lisbon, Greene tells us in the introduction to the Collected Edition, he had known German counter-espionage officers who sent home completely erroneous reports based on information received from imaginary agents, "It was a paying game," he tells us, "especially when expenses and bonuses were added to the cypher's salary, and a safe one. The fortunes of the German Government were now in decline, and it is wonderful how the concept of honor alters in the atmosphere of defeat."

Later in West Africa, Greene thought how easily he could have played the same game. In fact, he tells us of a report he filed on a Vichy airfield in French Guinea from an illiterate agent, who could not count above ten nor read a compass,"I had emphasized the agent's qualifications so that I was surprised when I earned a rating for his report of 'most valuable.' "

Early in the novel we encounter again the "lost childhood" motif when we are told, "childhood was the germ of all mistrust. You were cruelly joked upon and then you cruelly joked. You lost the remembrance of pain through inflicting it. But somehow, through no virtue of his own, he [Wormold] had never taken that course. Lack of character perhaps." When Wormold finally does show character and return a joke, it is at the expense of the British Secret Service.

The story is set in the years just prior to the overthrow of Battista by Castro and his rebels. A secret service agent named Hawthorne recruits a vacuum-cleaner salesman, James Wormold, for the Service, without much concern about whether Wormold wishes to be their "man in Havana." As it happens, the docile Wormold is in need of extra money to satisfy the demands of his lovely daughter, Milly, and Hawthorne's pushiness and appeal to Wormold's British citizenry are enough to launch the latter on a career whose complexity mushrooms.

Once Wormold accepts money for his services, he feels obliged to furnish weekly reports and turns to *Time*, which has a lengthy section on Cuba. The secret service seems accustomed to receiving from its sources information that is common knowledge but that it will not trust unless it comes from one of its sources. Thus *Time* and local newspapers stand Wormold in good stead for a while. Then, however, the apartment of his old friend, Dr. Hasselbacher, is ransacked, Wormold believes, by British agents because Hawthorne has said his German ancestry makes him suspect. Actually, Hasselbacher's apartment was invaded by counter-agents who wished him to spy on Wormold.

The injustice to Hasselbacher infuriates Wormold, who decides he will no longer play the game with a half a heart. He fabricates information about military installations under construction in Oriente Province, which seem too massive to be aimed at rebels. He even supplies drawings, which are in fact drawings of his Atomic Pile Vacuum Cleaner.

The romantic Chief of the Secret Service in London swallows everything Wormold sends him, and Wormold begins to receive salaries for the subagents he is expected to enlist. He enlists these "recruits," without their knowing it, from the country-club list, and adds to them an exotic dancer and a fictitious pilot, Raul Dominguez, who will explore the military installations for him. Once London sends Beatrice Severn to be his secretary, Wormold becomes still more adept at imaginative schemes and evasions. Fortunately he is helped by her lack of Spanish. Her superior thought that since she spoke French, another Latin tongue, she would do, and since Beatrice is a madcap, the superior is happy to be rid of her.

The humor turns grim when enemy secret service agents begin to take Wormold seriously, force Hasselbacher, an expert cryptographer, to decode his messages, kill a very real pilot coincidentally named Raul Dominguez, and shoot at Cifuentes, an unsuspecting "sub-agent" of Wormold. Wormold is thus forced to warn his other subagents, who have no idea of the capacity in which they serve, and we enjoy raucous scenes in which Wormold and Beatrice kidnap the exotic dancer, Teresa, sans clothing, and enter the house of another subagent, Prof. Sanchez, who is entertaining a mistress, misunderstands Wormold's mission, and meets him with a gun. When the enemy try to poison Wormold, Hasselbacher warns him and is himself killed. The farce has become an absurdist nightmare.

Wormold eventually confesses to Beatrice, who loves him more for his honesty, for his love of his daughter, and for his inventiveness than she liked him as a secret agent. To make one real contribution, Wormold secures the list of enemy names from the police captain, Segura, after a game of checkers with miniature whisky bottles as pieces. The rules of the game call for the player taking a piece to drink the contents of the bottle. Since Segura is the better player, this natural handicap works, forces Segura to pass out and enables Wormold to microphotograph the list and send it to England under a postage stamp.

Unfortunately, Wormold forgets which of the 500 letters he sends, according to emergency directions, has the crucial stamp. Thus the secret service is forced to soak 482 stamps before finding the list, which turns out to be illegible because Wormold had either overexposed the film or used the wrong side of the camera.

Wormold is brought back to England to face the music, and finds instead that he is to be awarded the O.B.E. since for the secret service to do otherwise would be to admit to the world that they had been duped. Wormold is put on the instructional staff, dealing with how to operate a station abroad, and he and Beatrice prepare for the future as he sends Milly abroad to finishing school with the money paid him by the secret service.

However light this "entertainment" seems, the reader recognizes once again why it transcends the spy-thriller genre. Greene's values are integrated into the story. Nowhere perhaps, and certainly not in the "entertainments," do we find so explicit a defense of "the virtue of disloyalty" until we come to *The Human Factor*. Wormold does not owe the loyalty to his country, whatever the entity may be, that he owes to his loved ones: Milly, Hasselbacher, Beatrice, himself. When Beatrice learns that he has been duping Hawthorne and Company, she enjoys the fact that he is "crazy" like herself. He is surprised:

> "Haven't you any more loyalty than I have?"
> "You are loyal."
> "Who to?"
> "To Milly, I don't care a damn about men who are loyal to the people who pay them, to organizations. . . . I don't think even my country means all that much. There are many countries in our blood —aren't there?— but only one person. Would the world be in the mess it is if we were loyal to love and not to countries?"

We are tempted to think Greene has done a *volte face* since *The Ministry of Fear*. It is true that much of the wartime nationalism of that novel has gone, but supranationalism has not replaced it. Beatrice serves as Wormold's spokesman before his superiors and, when he arrives in England, recapitulates for him:

"'What do you mean by his country? A flag someone invented two hundred years ago? The Bench of Bishops arguing about divorce and the House of Commons shouting Ya at each other across the floor? Or do you mean the T.U.C. and British Railways and the Co-Op? You probably think it's your regiment if you ever stop to think, but we haven't got a regiment—he and I.' They tried to interrupt and I said, 'Oh, I forgot—there's something greater than one's country, isn't there? You taught us that with your League of Nations and your Atlantic Pact, NATO and UNO and SEATO. But they don't mean any more to most of us than all the other letters, USA and USSR. And we don't believe you anymore when you say you want peace and justice and freedom. What kind of freedom? You want your careers.' I said I sympathized with the French officers in 1940 who looked after their families; they didn't anyway put their careers first. A country is more a family than a Parliamentary system."

Beatrice does not believe all that she says, and the case for disloyalty is not so convincingly made as it will be in *The Human Factor* since the prime reasons for disloyalty, Milly's needs and the attack on Hasselbacher, are not so weighty as the reasons offered in the later book. Still it is an argument Beatrice essentially believes, and that the author as well would seem to believe.

The reader might reasonably ask why I identify the opinions of author and characters here when I objected to others doing so in *The Quiet American*. The reasons are: one, that Greene has made himself explicit on the writer's "virtue of disloyalty"; two, that, not merely in this novel but in several novels we have considered and will consider, Greene uses his characters as vehicles (dramatically realized vehicles, but vehicles nonetheless) for the writer's "virtue of disloyalty"; and, three, in the case of Fowler, unlike that of Wormold or Beatrice, Greene showed his putative spokesman to represent a wrong view of life.

Not only are the author's values fleshed out in the story, then, and for the most part dramatically, but a whole host of characters comes to life, and this too sets the novel off from the standard thriller. Perhaps more characters than in *The Ministry of Fear* come vividly to life in the pages of this "entertainment."

Wormold is complex enough that director Carol Reed and Alec Guiness could not quite agree on how to play him in the film rendition of the novel. This timid vacuum salesman is essentially a sad clown. The novel's motto was taken from George Herbert, " And the sad man is cock of all his jests." The big kids cruelly joke and hurt his friends, so he has the last laugh. Hyperbolic as the story becomes, Wormold's motivation seems genuine, and he is clearly an original. Both Hasselbacher, as the long-standing, foreign friend, who still formally calls Wormold Mister, and Segura, as the sadistic police captain, who falls for young Milly, are nicely realized. We believe in Hasselbacher's romantic attachment to a military uniform used for parade and not for war, and in his human frailty when forced to decode Wormold's messages. Hasselbacher had been modeled on Baron Schacht, a friend of Norman Douglas, who lived in Capri. Like Hasselbacher, Schacht donned his now too small uniform every year on the Kaiser's birthday. Obviously the baron remained very alive in Greene's memory.

We believe in Segura, who is never quite mean enough to be a villain, who believes in a tortureable class that expects torture and an untortureable class that does not, whose wallet of human skin proves finally to be the skin of a police officer that tortured his father to death, who is kind to Wormold because of his love of Milly, and who "wasn't a bad chap . . . but not right for a husband." Segura seems to have been somewhat softened or humanized from Battista's notorious police chief, Captain Ventura, who served in part as his model.

Beatrice comes alive occasionally, as in her squirting Segura with soda water when he intrudes on Milly's birthday party or in her purchase of an enormous safe for Wormold's espionage materials as half of Havana looks on—"The only way to really become conspicuous is to try to escape notice."

At other times Beatrice seems only faintly realized and merely intended to serve the plot or to defend Wormold's higher loyalty. Milly is perhaps better drawn, combining Wormold's "crazy" side and a convent-school propriety. Her act of setting her thirteen-year-old classmate, Thomas Earl Parkman, on fire for pulling her hair shocks her father but later exhilarates him when he decides to "set fire" to the bothersome secret service. Milly had explained her action by saying, "I was tempted by the devil," and throughout she is a mixture of childish pietisms and mature perceptions. She embodies effectively and humorously the complexities of the adolescent.

The tone of this novel is so very different from that of the earlier novels that the regular reader of Greene is initially surprised. From the second chapter on, when the reader begins to get a glimpse of this young savage, Milly, in convent school, he or she is in a world more like Evelyn Waugh's than like early Greene's. "Milly was her home name: her given name was Seraphina—in Cuba a 'double of the second class,' a mysterious phrase which reminded Wormold of the race track."

Milly buys saddle, bridle and bit for a horse she *knows* her father will buy her since she has made two novenas for it. Wormold hopelessly asks, "Where's the horse?" and half expects it to appear in the bathroom. Hawthorne's first overtures to Wormold, having him come into the men's room and talk over running water when they had the privacy of an empty bar, are farcical. The interludes in London in which the Chief imagines this vacuum salesman an old-time "merchant adventurer" are equally farcical. Wormold's use of *Time* for information, his botching his one positive act of microphotographing, and his being rewarded with an O.B.E. and an instructional post create an atmosphere akin to nothing in earlier Greene.

However, the novel never becomes so much a farce that its meaning is lost. The unreasonable demands made by ths secret service upon personal loyalties in the interest of some narrowly national higher loyalty is as effectively satirized in this tone as German loyalty and supranationalism are attacked in *The Ministry of Fear's* quite different tone. The novel's meaning is guaranteed by the sudden break in humor when a real Raul Dominguez is killed and when Dr. Hasselbacher is murdered in a colossal, adolescent game.

The danger here was that Greene would not be able to resume the light tone. However, Raul's death is forgotten (we had not known him anyway) in the hilarious scene in which Wormold goes to warn his unsuspecting strip-teaser. Hasselbacher's death is a more serious problem and a heavier tone is maintained for several chapters after that point. What serves as an effective transition back to a light tone is the checkers game with whisky bottles. This scene is both deadly serious and comic, and the latter tone ultimately emerges.

The novel, then, is an effective comedy, meant to do more than entertain and eminently successful in its intention. It is no surprise that Greene henceforth found more room for comedy in his novels.

Chapter Eleven

## *A BURNT-OUT CASE* (1961)

In *A Burnt-Out Case*, Greene partly returns to a religious theme, and his critics return to an identification of author and character. Though Greene uses a third-person narrator, and not the first-person of *The Quiet American*, even so sympathetic a friend as Evelyn Waugh thought now of Greene as the "Lost Leader." After a look at the story and at Greene's method, perhaps we can put this continuous identification to a permanent rest. Perhaps too we can put to rest the notion that Greene's later novels signal a loss of religious faith.

M. Querry, a Church architect of international repute, has left Europe and come to this remote leper colony in the French Congo. He has lost interest in his work because it is not understood by the people who use his churches, who vulgarize his work with saccharine statuary and gaudy stained-glass. He has also discovered that he built for his own glory, a glory that is no longer rewarding to him. He has lost his religious faith and he does not find any satisfaction in his personal life, which had been a series of loves unrequited by him but meant to indulge his vanity. Unable now to feel anything, love or hate, Querry has come to Africa to escape.

To Querry's chagrin, a bizzare and pietistic colonial merchant, M. Rycker, insists on seeing him as a kind of desert father, retreating from the world to seek sanctity. One of the more naive priests at the leproserie, Father Thomas, encourages such a view, referring in mystical terms to Querry's *noche oscura*. Rycker succeeds in bringing to the Congo Montagu Parkinson, a literary hack, who proceeds to write a fantastic story of conversion for *Paris Dimanche*. Interested in preserving his retreat from the world, Querry angrily comes to silence Rycker, finds him sick and his young wife petrified that she may be pregnant and will enrage Rycker by such carelessness. Querry gives her a ride to the doctor's and they are forced to stay overnight, in adjoining hotel rooms, to await the result of her rabbit test.

When Querry thinks Marie Rycker is crying in her room, he comes to her and passes most of the evening telling her a story intended to make her sleep. Tongue in-cheek, Marie enters in her diary that she spent the night with Querry. Then partly through fear of her husband's reaction to a child and partly through fascination for Querry, Marie fantasizes that the baby is Querry's. It was, after all, conceived some months before when Querry stayed with them and when, forced to make love to her husband, she pretended he was Querry.

Marie goes so far as to lie to her husband, who, prepared with the suspicions of Parkinson, who has seen them together at the hotel, believes Querry guilty. After a scene in which Querry tells Rycker he is wrong, in which Querry is even forced to say he is not attracted to Marie, Rycker is even more insulted by what he thinks Querry's haughtiness. He returns home and comes a few days later to the leper colony, where he shoots Querry to death. Thus Querry dies for an offense he had not committed, having earlier in his life escaped judgment for those he had.

Knowing the story, we can return to the nagging problem of critics reading character as author. It is true that Greene was fed up at this time with Christians trying to use him as a guru or father confessor. Between the success of *The Heart of the Matter* and *The End of the Affair*, Greene tells us in his introduction to the Collected Edition, he felt himself "used and exhausted by the victims of religion. The vision of faith as an untroubled sea was lost for ever." He had been telephoned and written by countless people seeking his spiritual advice, and he seems to have felt that the Church was not helping its sufferers. This feeling, combined with his growing distaste for "moral theology" seems to have produced Querry.

The same year that Greene published the present novel he published also *In Search of a Character*, as we saw in Chapter One. In this journal of his trip into the Congo, Greene tells of the model for his clerical captain of the boat that brought Querry down the Congo. The priest in the story and in the journal would shoot his rifle at any animal he could, heron, eagle, alligator, "Now it's a heron and alas! this time the captain's aim is true. It flaps and tries to rise and sinks into the water. The boat is put about. I can't help remebering the late Cardinal Griffin at a dinner at Dick Stoke's opposing a Blood Sports Bill which was under discussion on the ground that animals were created for man's pleasure as well as for his use." Then Greene adds in a footnote displaying a tone very uncharacteristic of him, "And if that is a correct view of moral theology, to hell I would say with moral theology."

This anger with moral theology, and with dogmatic theology too, is seen several times in *A Burnt-Out Case*. Rycker, of course, is the expert at moral theology and uses it to browbeat his wife. Dr. Colin, discussing the natives' strange mixture of Christianity and paganism, remarks, "It's a strange Christianity we have here, but I wonder whether the Apostles would find it as difficult to understand as the collected works of Thomas Aquinas. If Peter could have understood those, it would have been a greater miracle than Pentecost, don't you think? Even the Nicean Creed—it has the flavour of higher mathematics to me." The fathers are closer to Dr. Colin than to Rycker in their views. When the narrator tells of the promiscuity of these mutilated lepers and the resulting offspring brought for baptism, he goes on to say, "The fathers were too busy to bother themselves with what the Church considered sin (moral theology was the subject they were least concerned with)."

These reservations about moral theology that all the well-balanced characters in the novel have do perhaps reflect a change in Greene. However, a reluctance to accept traditional answers and a frustration with a Church that too frequently offers such answers to a laity that accepts them but is not really touched by them does not add up to a renunciation of faith. Greene's sentiments do not equate him with Querry, and he asks Waugh, "Must a Catholic be forbidden to paint the portrait of a lapsed Catholic? Undoubtedly if there is any realism in the character it must come from the author experiencing some of the same moods as Querry, but surely and not necessarily, with the sane intensity... If people are so impetuous as to regard the book as a recantation of faith I cannot help it. Perhaps they will be surprised to see me at Mass."

Greene's method is that of any novelist. He uses material from personal experience. He enters into his characters as fully as possible. His most successful characters, like the most successful characters of Dickens, are those into whom he can enter most fully, those who share some of the author's sentiments.

Apart from some of Querry's theological sentiments coinciding with Greene's, the major reason for critics identifying Greene and Querry is Querry's being an architect. He too is a creator. However, Greene's journal tells us that the novel was forming in his head before he went to Africa, and he did not think of making Querry an architect until he had been there a while, saw a priest in charge of construction, and apparently realized it would be a way of giving his character something to do in the leper colony. In an interesting entry a week later, Greene tells us of men standing in pirogues in the water so that they have the appearance of wading. Then he asks, "Has some rationalist suggested this as an explanation of Christ walking upon the water?" Greene then places this *rationalist* reflection in the mouth of Querry in the novel.

I have dwelt at some length on the confusion of author and character not because it is itself important whether Greene's politics are Fowler's or his religion Querry's, but because the confusion detracts from his art. If a reader cannot see how effectively Greene can empathize with a viewpoint, with several viewpoints, not his own, but thinks Greene writes autobiography, he will fail to understand and appreciate the novelist's creativity.

To return to the novel itself, we note that the parallel between physical leprosy and spiritual leprosy is reasonably effective. Such an analogy helps weave the author's values into the text somewhat implicitly. Querry's servant, Deo Gratias, progresses from a contagious leper to a burnt-out case. He no longer has hands or feet, but he is cured, except perhaps psychologically. "Now that a cure had been found for the physical disease, he [Dr. Colin] had always to remember that leprosy remained a psychological problem." Likewise, Querry moves from his state of spiritual leprosy, from his selfish, vain, unfeeling condition to a state in which his sickness has been arrested. He recklessly goes into the bush at night and saves Deo Gratias, sleeping with and protecting him through the night. When Querry later shows concern over another leper, Dr. Colin thinks he may be cured, may be a burnt-out case.

With the partial return of spiritual health, Querry paradoxically brings about his own death. When he had first arrived at the leper colony, he could not tolerate the unsubtle, childish humor of the priests as they played cards for matchsticks. By story's end, however, Querry had regained his humor. At the champagne party celebrating the new hospital, he reflects how "he had walked out into the bush unable to bear their laughter and their infantility. How was it that he could now sit here and smile with them? He even found himself resenting the strict face of Father Thomas, who sat at the end of the table unamused."

However, when Querry laughs in the presence of the enraged Rycker, the latter thinks Querry laughs arrogantly and kills him. Brother Phillipe is trying to get Rycker to put away the gun and come into the mission:

> "Please come to the mission, M. Rycker," Brother Phillipe pleaded. "We'll put up a bed for you there. We shall all of us feel better after a night's sleep. And a cold shower in the morning," he added, and as though to illustrate his words a waterfall of rain suddenly descended on them. Querry made an odd awkward sound which the doctor by now had learned to interpret as a laugh, and Rycker fired twice. The lamp fell with Querry and smashed; the burning wick flared up once under the deluge of rain, lighting an open mouth and a pair of surprised eyes, and then went out.

Querry's last words are an attempt to let Rycker know he was not laughing at him.

Effective a central symbol as leprosy is, the parallel between leprosy and sickness of soul is too limited to serve as a vehicle for allegory, and the novel seems to rely for its meaning on more talk than does *The Heart of the Matter* or *The Power and the Glory*.

Most of the purposeful talk is between the novel's two best realized characters, Querry and Dr. Colin. M. Rycker is too stereotyped a religious hypocrite and Greene, in a fine simile, seems almost to have intended the stereotype, "But Rycker was like a wall so plastered over with church-announcements that you couldn't even see the brickwork behind."

Father Thomas too is flat, a narrow, pietistic, unloving and unloved man. His adulation of Querry and quick turnabout at Rycker's first accusation are the actions of a shallow prude. Only Querry and Colin come alive, and only their talk interests us.

The journalist, Parkinson, who gets his facts and his quotations wrong, does not care to get them right. He chooses to give his readers what they want, and what they want is that Querry be a modern-day Augustine or Damian. Parkinson's complete disregard for truth joins him in self-deception with Rycker and Father Thomas. Parkinson had come to believe his own lies, "I'm disappointed in you, Querry. I'd begun to believe my own story about you." All three turn on Querry as quickly and unreasonably as they had turned to him. A reader has to go back almost to Hall in *England Made Me* or to Pinkie in *Brighton Rock* to find characters so little deserving of sympathy in Greene. And here we have three of them. Such a phenomenon can perhaps only be explained by Greene's concern for truth. He has repeatedly said that his intention is that his writing be truthful in both substance and form.[1] Parkinson is the antithesis of what Greene believes the writer ought to be, and Rycker and Father Thomas are his counterparts in the world of business and the world of religion. Though at first it might seem ironic that the most "orthodox" of the fathers is given the doubter's name, it is not ironic in the least. The others respond to the mystery of Christ. Thomas needs to see and touch with his hands before he will believe anything.

Marie Rycker does not sufficiently come alive even to be a type. The one moment we see her best is as she tells Querry he really did "father" her child since it was conceived as she pretended Rycker was Querry. With this piece of self-seduction, she leaves the story. In the last analysis, she seems another version of Pyle, the destructive innocent.

Dr. Colin is a dedicated and loving man, an atheist who does as much for the lepers as do any of the priests. When Querry refers to Colin and himself as atheists, Colin does not believe Querry qualifies. Thinking he must leave the Congo, Querry remarks,

> "We would have made an atheist corner between us."
> "I wonder if you would have qualified for that."
> "Why not?"
> "You're too troubled by your lack of faith, Querry.

> You keep on fingering it like a sore you want to get rid of. I am content with the myth; you are not—you have to believe or disbelieve."

Querry follows this up immediately by saying, "Somebody is calling out there. I thought for a moment it was my name." Querry's words refer to Rycker, who is searching for him, but they are meant by the narrator to suggest more than Rycker, and implicitly to corroborate Colin's view of Querry.

In his introduction, Greene tells us he was happy with his depiction of Dr. Colin, and when he referred to Colin's "easy atheism" in a letter to Evelyn Waugh, the latter took issue with the phrase, thinking it only superficially possible for an atheist to be at ease. Less sympathetic than Greene with atheism, Waugh found that atheists occupy the "waste land" that Greene reserved for "pious suburbans." Greene referred in this phrase not to the piety of the simple but to that of Catholics who have ceased to look for God because they assume they have found and possess Him. It is, of course, Greene's sympathy with the atheistic viewpoint that enables him to bring to life a character whose view of life differs from his own.

Colin and Querry are complementary in many ways. Unlike Querry who built churches to a God in whom he had little belief and for people whom he despised, Colin believes in no God but gives himself freely to the mankind in whom he does believe. If Colin has any transcendent belief, it is in evolution, not merely in evolution of the body but, like the Jesuit anthropologist, Teilhard de Chardin, in an evolution of the spirit as well. Christ was really a "fertile element" in that growth. When Querry calls such a belief as much superstition as the belief of the priests, Colin proves himself the believer in Pascal's gamble that so many of Greene's characters have been. "Who cares? It's the superstition I live by. There was another superstition—quite unproved—Copernicus had it the earth went round the sun. Without that superstition we shouldn't be in a position now to shoot rockets at the moon. One has to gamble on one's superstitions. As Pascal gambled on his."

When Colin tells Querry his only love in life is dead, Querry assumes Colin, like himself, has come to the leper colony to run away:

> "So that's why you came out here."
> "You are wrong," Colin said. "She's buried a hundred yards away. She was my wife."

Querry has never lived Colin's life of dedicated love, but, as he lives and works in the leper colony, he does in an inchoate way exemplify

Colin's belief that no human being entirely lacks love—though "sometimes . . . people call it hate." It is ironic, of course, that Querry cannot convince people that a builder of churches who gives it up to flee to the Congo is not necessarily giving up the world's pomp to seek sanctity in the wilds. Yet he is killed by these people at the first real signs of spiritual life in him.

Though Greene went to the Congo in search of his character, an old favorite, Browning, might ultimately have furnished the model in Fra Lippo Lippi. Like the poet's monologuist, Querry is contemptuous of the way Christians have used his art for pietistic purposes. As with Lippi too, the Christian myth furnishes his subject matter though he himself is only nominally Christian, and like Lippi's looking forward to his successor, Raphael, to improve upon him, Querry looks forward to his successor, who will not be a "spoilt priest."

The "spoilt priest" motif is pursued throughout the novel, and Querry even dreams of himself as a priest who has no sacramental wine for Mass, and when he locates some, has it snatched out from under him by another priest in need. As a "spoilt priest" Querry is a kind of symbol for all the failures in the novel. Querry calls Parkinson, who has turned his talent to hack journalism, a "spoilt priest." Rycker, who had six years in the Jesuit seminary, is also a spoilt priest, retaining only the trappings of Christianity, the chalice without the wine. And Father Thomas is in his way a spoilt priest. The atheist, Colin, is the only layman in the novel who is an unspoilt priest, and we recognize it in Father Superior's sermon, "He not believe in Yezu, but he a Klistian." The spoilt priest motif is a variation of the familiar divided-self obsession and to that obsession Greene adds another familiar one: the value of suffering in bringing the self together.

*In Search of a Character* shows that Greene originally intended to give his character just an initial to avoid narrow national associations in a name. However, to do this, he had learned from his *Confidential Agent*, was to start people talking about Kafka. Querry succeeds as a character because, though he has an allegorical dimension, he is sufficiently realized to be believed on a literal level. He can steal a woman from her boyfriend merely to serve his vanity, but he can also go into the bush after dark to rescue a poor leper. He lacks humor at first but possesses honesty. Ultimately this honesty enables him to see himself and sets him apart from the other spoilt priests in the story. We come to like Querry and, perhaps more important, to believe in him.

The novel's tone is far removed from that of the previous novel. However, it is not without humor. As Querry himself suggests, his story might easily have been a comedy entitled, *The Innocent Adulterer*. Since the novel is seen primarily from Querry's point of view and he takes a long time to learn to laugh, most of the comedy is of the dark variety. We can laugh at the Tartuffian fraud, Rycker, but his foolishness turns tragic. Perhaps the novel's only genuinely light moment occurs when Father Superior tries to have Mme. Rycker buy the Order some bidets, which he thinks are foot baths. The innocence of even the shrewdest of these priests is something that contrasts effectively with Querry's worldliness and something that Querry grows to like.

Most of the novel is told, as we have seen, in the third person, from Querry's point of view. Why? By seeing through his eyes, we are not as likely as Rycker or Father Thomas to romanticize. Nor are we likely to judge him as severely as they ultimately do. Only rarely is the focus of narration anyone else, as when we briefly see with Marie Rycker's eyes so that we might understand why her life would motivate her to tell the lies that implicate Querry. Or in the second chapter we see through Dr. Colin's eyes so that we will not first see the leper colony as a place where the work of God is marvellously going forward but as a place where God is to be questioned:

> For fifteen years the doctor had dreamt of a day when he would have funds available for constructing special tools to fit each mutilation, but now he hadn't money enough even to provide decent mattresses in the hospital.
> "What's your name?" he asked.
> "Deo Gratias."
> Impatiently the doctor called out the next number.

The bitter irony of the name sets the tone and also exemplifies something else about Greene's writing: how deftly he handles exposition. The leper's name and Colin's reaction tell us immediately something of the doctor's character. In chapter one, we learn about Querry just as naturally. The natives sing *ex tempore* chants in their own Mongo language. Querry asks the captain what they sing about him and the captain tells him:

> "Here is a white man who is neither a father nor a doctor. He has no beard. He comes from a long way away—we do not know from where—and he tells no one to what place he is going nor why. He is rich man, for he drinks whisky every evening and he smokes all the time. Yet he offers no man a cigarette."

It is an excellent device for telling us something about Querry and in keeping with the African custom of singing about the events and characters of a journey. Shortly thereafter, when Querry sees the men in the pirogue and suggests to the priest that might be how Christ walked on water, we are introduced to another side of his character.

The novel then displays many of Greene's finest qualities. Ultimately, however, its story is too thin, too focussed on the passive figure of Querry to engage us as do Greene's best novels. Though his fast style moves the reader along, we arrive at the end feeling little interest in Querry and convinced that the story leans too heavily on its final irony. Still that irony signals another kind of beginning in Greene. From now on he seems to view life as more comic than tragic, as a huge metaphysical joke that can often end in disaster. Still, though a story end in disaster, we wag our heads rather than weep. The death of Querry or the death of Plaar, in *The Honorary Consul*, is not treated in the same tragic tone as was the death of Scobie.

## Chapter Twelve

# *THE COMEDIANS* (1966)

Greene's first novel in five years resumes an old theme, the need for engagement. In his previous novel, *A Burnt-Out Case*, religious engagement—in a broad sense—was needed; in *The Quiet American*, political engagement was called for. Set in Duvalier's Haiti, *The Comedians* asks for one or the other: "Catholics and Communists have committed great crimes, but at least they have not stood aside like an established society, and been indifferent, Dr. Magiot writes to our narrator, Brown, who is very like the disengaged narrator of *The Quiet American*.

The established societies that stand aside are the capitalistic countries, particularly, in this case, the United States, which will implicitly approve any government that acts as a "bulwark against Communism." Thus, the novel criticizes political insensitivity once again.

When the story opens, passengers, very unlikely named Smith, Jones and Brown, are bound via the Dutch ship, Medea, from New York and Philadelphia to Port-au-Prince, Haiti. The half-French and half-English narrator. Brown, is returning to a hotel he owns and a mistress he does not; the American idealists, the Smiths, are bringing vegetarianism to Haiti; and a bogus British major named Jones comes for reasons no one is sure about, but which prove to be military adventure.

Brown resumes his affair with Martha Piñeda, wife of a South American ambassador. The Smiths use the fact that Mr. Smith was a presidential candidate in 1948 as an entree, yet experience nothing but disenchantment in their efforts to establish a vegetarian center in this terrorist republic. Jones, after being arrested upon entry for reasons of the general suspicion that followed him, uses his consummate charm to con even President Duvalier and his secret police, the Tontons Macoute.

Brown's love affair with Martha is impaired by his petty jealousies, of her son, of her husband, finally of Jones. When his phony military record is discovered by the Tontons Macoute, Jones is brought to Piñeda's embassy for asylum. Since Jones had been appealed to earlier by the poet-rebel, Philipot, to serve as the rebel's military instructor, Brown seizes upon the opportunity to expose the braggart to whom Martha, like everyone else, has taken a liking. In Martha's presence, he asks Jones whether he would be willing to be smuggled out of the embassy and into rebel territory. To Brown's surprise and Martha's disturbance, Jones readily accepts, and Brown brings him to Philipot's band of rebels. When the Tontons Macoute follow and capture Jones and Brown, the rebels come to their rescue and kill these secret police. Jones joins the rebels, and Brown crosses the border into Santo Domingo and safety.

The rebels are eventually routed, and Jones dies bravely while covering their escape. When Brown later asks Philipot about Jones' military abilities, Philipot has to admit he was "rusty" in certain matters, like firing a gun. But "he knew how to lead" and, perhaps more important, "the men loved him. He made them laugh." And these were men whose French he did not understand. Brown is left having played the poorest role of all, one of selfish detachment. Jones' braggadocio did commit him. The Smiths' absurd desire to reduce acidity and thus violence, among a starving, terrorized people involves them in almost heroic fashion. Dr. Magiot dies for his communism, and Philipot is beaten by his quixotic schemes. All were more successful comedians, playing more meaningful comic roles than did the detached narrator, Brown.

Greene called his characters "comedians" for two reasons, one because they all play a role in life that is more or less absurd; the other, allied to it, because life itself is more comic than tragic. Brown sounds that note early in the novel:

> When I was a boy I had faith in the Christian God. Life under his shadow was a very serious affair; I saw Him incarnated in every tragedy. He belonged to the *lacrimae rerum* like a gigantic figure looming through Scottish mist. Now that I approached the end of life it was only my sense of humour that enabled me sometimes to believe in Him. Life was a comedy, not the tragedy for which I had been prepared, and it seemed to me that we were all, on this boat with a Greek name (why would a Dutch line name its boats in Greek?) driven by an authoritative practical joker towards the extreme point of comedy. How often, in the crowd on Shaftesbury Avenue or Broadway, after the theatres closed, have I heard the phrase—"I laughed till the tears came."

Among these comedians, however, there is a wide range of importance, of dignity, even of heroism salvaged through their respective roles. The Smiths are seen by the narrator as absurd in applying vegetarian solutions to Haiti's problems. They naively overrate the "coloured man," expecting to find in him virtues his white counterpart lacks. Yet in practice the Smiths behave toward all their fellows with kindness and dignity. When the black regime encourages the vegetarian center only for their share in the rake-off they are certain these Americans must intend, the Smiths finally reject Haiti for Santo Domingo. Their idealism wins Brown's admiration:

> "Perhaps we seem rather comic figures to you, Mr. Brown."
> "Not comic," I said in sincerity, "heroic."

Brown's respect for Jones develops more slowly and grudgingly. Jones is not naive, but he is a braggart and, Brown intuits from the first, no military man. The idea of this victim of self-fantasy becoming Haiti's Castro is made even more impossible for Brown to accept because he is jealous of Martha's liking for Jones. Still Jones' ability to con people proves due to his charming humor and reckless heroism, and Brown himself eventually falls victim to these qualities.

Brown is the least successful comedian because he throws himself into no role. He chooses to be a spectator and spends his time making love to the ambassador's wife. He is the first character since the lost Pinkie in *Brighton Rock* to whom Greene gives the expression, *Dona nobis pacem*. And like Pinkie, Brown is not to be granted that peace, surely not in making love to Mrs. Piñeda. In an effectively written love scene, the author makes this clear with metaphoric indirection. Martha says to Brown:

> "We aren't concerned.
> "No. We wouldn't make very good rebels, you and I.
> "I don't imagine Joseph will either. With that damaged hip.
> "Or Philipot without his Bren. I wonder if he's got Baudelaire in his breast-pocket to stop the bullets. Don't be too hard on me then," she said, because I'm German and the Germans did nothing." She moved her hand as she spoke and my desire came back, so that I didn't bother to ask her what she meant. Not with Luis safely away in South America and Angel occupied with his puzzles and the Smiths out of sight and hearing. I could imagine the taste of milk on her breasts and the taste of honey between her thighs. I could imagine for a moment that I was entering the promised land, but the spasm of hope was soon over, and she spoke as though her thoughts had not for a moment left their furrow. She said, "Haven't

the French a word for going into the streets?"
"My mother must have gone into the streets I suppose, unless it was her lover who gave her the Resistance medal."
"My father went into the streets too in 1930, but he became a war criminal. Action is dangerous, isn't it?"

The lesser characters are also comedians. The poet, Philipot, leads the rebels with machine guns from the Capone era. The gifted Dr. Magiot acts as their contact. Though she denies her comic role, Martha Piñeda plays the part of a loving wife and mother while conducting an affair with Brown. Even the Tontons Macoute wear masks, their dark glasses, meant not only to intimidate but to hide their own fears and uncertainties as well. Petit Pierre the gossip columnist goes about with a perpetual smile on his face except, Brown notes, when the blackout is momentarily interrupted and the lights suddenly turned on. Petit Pierre's smile is perhaps the dominant symbol in the novel, "His gay manner did not necessarily mean good news, for Petit Pierre was always gay. It was as though he had tossed a coin to decide between the only two possible attitudes in Port-au-Prince, the rational and the irrational, misery or gaiety; Papa Doc's head had fallen earthwards and he had plumped for the gaiety of despair."

If Petit Pierre serves as one kind of symbol in the novel, a phrase from Horace serves as another. *Exegi monumentum aere perennis* (I have completed a monument more lasting than bronze.) is a phrase recollected by Brown from his schooldays with the Jesuits. The monument primarily referred to is the one that Brown builds to Jones via this story he narrates or the one that Jones' life creates in his own memory. It is in connection with Jones that the narrator first uses the expression. When he uses it again, Brown is thinking of his hotel, the *Trianon.* Yet it is a hotel he never built and one he must finally surrender.

Of course, everyone in the story builds a monument of some kind to himself through the role he or she enacts and the narrator immortalizes. The Smiths' monument is as noble as that of Jones. Contrasted with these living monuments, Brown's may be suggested at the story's end when he becomes a mortician's assistant.

Another of the novel's motifs is suggested in the repeated phrase, *prêtre manqué*. Like Querry of *A Burnt-Out Case*, Brown is called a spoilt priest. The phrase refers not merely to Brown's youthful flirtation with a religious vocation but also, as with several characters discussed in the earlier novel, to his abandoning of any vocation that would serve God and his fellow man.

Apart from the novel's real success in dramatizing imaginatively man's need for involvement, it is a remarkable success in the creation of characters. A host of vivid characters, possibly more than in any previous Greene novel, people the story. Jones, Mr. and Mrs. Smith, Dr. Magiot all possess the capacity to surprise us that E. M. Forester calls the test of a round character. Most of the lesser characters too are vividly drawn for their limited roles in advancing the story. Brown's mother, Comtesse de Lascot-Villiers, is a character who anticipates the delightful Aunt Augusta of Greene's next novel. The captain of the *Medea* is a straightlaced legalist seemingly borrowed right from the captain of the Sephora in Conrad's "Secret Sharer." Yet Greene's captain surprises with a strength of character that same captain did not have when he disarms the Tontons Macoute who board his ship in search of Jones. In retrospect, however, we find the action perfectly consistent with his former stringency.

Capt. Concasser, the one member of the Tontons Macoute we come to know, shows an insecurity, fear, and human quality behind those dark glasses that make him more than a stereotyped bully. Martha too shows a humanity her lover does not as she comes vividly before us in several passages, perhaps most when she chastises Brown for his selfish jealousy of Jones. He tells her that they will "have peace together when he's gone. You won't be torn in two between us then."

> She looked at me a moment as though I had said something that shocked her. Then she came up to the bed and took my hand as though I were a child who didn't understand the meaning of his words but who must be warned all the same not to repeat them. She said, "My darling, be careful. Don't you understand? To you nothing exists except in your own thoughts. Not me, not Jones. We're what you choose to make us. You're a Berkeleyan. My God, what a Berkeleyan. You've turned poor Jones into a seducer and me into a woman mistress. You can't even believe in your mother's medal, can you? You've written her a different part. My dear, try to believe we exist when you aren't there. We're independent of you. None of us is like you fancy we are. Perhaps it wouldn't matter much if your thoughts were not so dark, always so dark."

This kind of anti-Berkeleyism is a favorite theme of Greene's, but here it comes quite appropriately from Martha's lips. As narrator, Brown has a little of the predictability of David Copperfield, but it does not matter significantly since it's the other comedians in whose roles we find enjoyment and a certain ironic truth.

Greene's use of a first-person narrator for the third time seems best since we are not interested in Brown's life even as much as we were in Copperfield's. It is the Micawbers and Steerforths of this story that fascinate us. Brown's passivity is best seen as a contrast to the involvement of the other characters.

The novel was made into a film in 1967. So many Greene novels have been so adapted that Stanley Kauffmann refers to them as a genre in themselves.[1] The film had an extraordinary cast, with Alec Guinness as Jones, Richard Burton as Brown, and Paul Ford and Lillian Gish as the Smiths. In addition. Peter Ustinov played Piñeda, Elizabeth Taylor Martha Piñeda, and James Earl Jones Dr. Magiot. Several critics praised Ustinov, and that very praise is indicative of the kinds of changes the film made. Piñeda was not only a larger character but a more attractive one in the film. Greene tells us that this was necessary since the film could not be presented through the book's narrator, Brown, who disliked Piñeda.

Another accommodation was that Greene could not use flashbacks in an already lengthy film (2 hours 40 minutes) to explain Brown's youth. He was dependent on dialogue for such explanation. Furthermore, the film had to be made in color. For a novel in which darkness is stressed to create a mood, color is simply not appropriate.

Perhaps the greatest change is that the film moralized more than the novel. Writing for *America*, Moira Walsh saw the film's concern as "exploring the exploitation of the poor." In fact, the same reviewer saw Greene's film as pessimistically concluding one evil dictatorship would inevitably be replaced by another.[2] The novel's primary theme of commitment seems to have been overwhelmed by the more cinematically visible social issue.

Whatever its own merits, Peter Glenville's film could not give the reader of Greene what the novel offered. Without the same point of view and structure, without quite the same mood and even story, the viewer had to put aside his knowledge of the novel and enjoy a terrain that offered some similar landmarks.

## Chapter Thirteen

## *TRAVELS WITH MY AUNT* (1969)

In 1969 Greene published *Travels With My Aunt*, a novel different from anything he had previously written. Its hilarious tone had been anticipated in *Our Man in Havana*, but that novel belonged to the genre of Greene spy thrillers. *Travels With My Aunt*, on the other hand, is an unusual *Bildungsroman*, in which the growing up of its protagonist begins belatedly in middle age when he meets his real mother at the funeral of his putative mother. The stuffy Henry Pulling drops his dahlias and quiet retirement and enters a mad-cap life with "Aunt Augusta," finally taking control of her business, smuggling whisky in Paraguay and Argentina. In the process, however, of being pulled kicking into life, Henry finds himself unwittingly smuggling currency, smoking pot, resisting Turkish police, being arrested for blowing his nose in a party flag in Paraguay, and finally marrying a Paraguayan girl as soon as she turns sixteen.

At one point in his travels with Augusta, Henry felt as though he "were being dragged at her heels in an absurd knight-errantry, like Sancho Panza at the heels of Don Quixote, but in the cause of what she called fun instead of chivalry." The novel is, in fact, as much an English adaptation of Cervantes classic as was Dickens' *Pickwick Papers*. Like Sancho, Henry can see nothing in life but the glaringly obvious as his aunt leads him about: his lawnmower getting rusted by the rain, his dahlias not being cared for, his likelihood of being thrown into prison. He cannot see beyond the routine, in which he has imprisoned himself, to the zestful life Aunt Augusta lives and offers to him. His is a humorously handled, but extreme case of "lost childhood."

Once again Greene employs a first-person narrator, and the choice is excellent, almost necessary. Henry Pulling criticizes Augusta's unconventionality and, as the author intends, we side with her. We find the narrator simply too stuffy. Nowhere is our attitude toward him more formed than in his own attitude toward travel: "Travel could be a great waste of time. This was the hour of the early evening when the sun had lost its heat and the shadows fell across my small lawn, the hour when I would take my yellow watering-can and fill it from the garden tap . . ." Or when he learns his aunt plans to take him for a little sea air—to Istanbul: "It was weak of me, but I did not then realize the depth of my aunt's passion for travel. If I had I would have hesitated before I made the first fatal proposal, 'I have nothing to do today. If you would like to go to Brighton . . .'"

The point of view serves its purpose. Had Greene used third person, the reader might have felt the author was too obviously building a case for Augusta's unconventionality at the expense of Henry's conventionality. As it is, irony serves the purpose of having us laugh at Henry and sympathize with Augusta. By indirection we are won, as is Henry eventually, to Augusta's *joie de vivre*.

Another purpose served by the point of view is pace. The stodgy narrator slows us down, prevents madcap adventures from mounting too rapidly and causing our interest to fade. The film version of the novel exemplifies what Greene's narrator enabled the novel to avoid. The considerable talent of director George Cukor and actress Maggie Smith could not keep audience attention long. We experience Aunt Augusta too directly, too many of her zany adventures come in rapid succession, and Maggie Smith gives what Moira Walsh, writing for *America*, appropriately called a "too hyperthyroid" performance.[1] The fault is not Miss Smith's. She has played more demanding roles brilliantly. The fault lies again in the transfer of story from one medium to another. The same point of view does not operate in the film to slow the pace.

I mentioned the hilarity of the novel, but it would be wrong to overemphasize it. An equally poignant tone operates implicitly throughout. The scene in which Henry Pulling eats his Christmas meal at his favorite restaurant, at a table separate from the Admiral and from Major Charge, while a piece of mistletoe hangs "in an undangerous position over the toilet" is sad enough to border on sentimentality. In fact, the reader might find sentimental the scene at the "West Berlin Hotel" in Istanbul where everyone joins in the dance but Henry. He is moved to a moment of introspection. "I was drunk, I knew that, for drunken tears stood in my eyes, and I wanted to throw my beer glass on the floor and join the dancing. But I was excluded, as I had always been excluded."

The sadness implicit throughout is the sadness of Wordsworth's "Intimations Ode." Greene has alluded to this poem in several of his novels, but nowhere more than in *Travels With My Aunt*. Wordsworth, as Augusta calls her black lover, is a "happy shepherd boy" like the young boy of the poem, and Henry contrasts sharply with him. The reader may remember that Wordsworth's poem speculates on the intense aliveness, wonder, sensual pleasure we enjoy when young. Where does it come from? Unlike Plato, who thinks of the "prison house" of the body closing on the soul and removing memory of previous existence, Wordsworth follows the Neoplatonists in seeing the prison house of custom closing on the spirit gradually and removing recollection of that other perfect world we have come from. Custom, then, robs us of the joys of youth. Thus, Henry is no longer the happy shepherd boy that the novel's Wordsworth is. And Henry is not the only victim. When he reads his father's copy of Palgrave's *Golden Treasury*, he remarks: "Thus when I first entered the bank a junior clerk I thought of it in Wordsworth's terms as a 'prison house'—what was it my father had found a prison, so that he double-marked the passage? Perhaps our home, and my stepmother and I had been the warders." Henry surmises correctly. His father married, not Henry's mother—Augusta, but her sister, Angelica, who locked herself and her two men in a prison.

Custom will not imprison Augusta, who lives with as much variety as Henry's Uncle Jo. That uncle, Aunt Augusta tells us, acquired a fifty-two bedroom house so that he could live a week in each room (He had originally tried for a 365 room house!). Life does not rush by in a blur if you change locations frequently. Uncle Joe died in transit on the bathroom floor, while dragging himself off his deathbed and moving with valise to the next room. And so, Aunt Augusta's stories and adventures keep the Wordsworthian nostalgia from ever becoming the dominant tone.

Augusta is surely one of the best depicted women in Greene's canon. The author again demonstrates that he can create a full-bodied, vibrant woman, as he had in Sarah Miles or Kate Farrant. Augusta is more than a madcap. She is a woman whose life has had its tragic side. She could not marry Henry's father, whom she loved; her inheritance had been squandered by another lover, Visconti; she was ostracized by her family and deprived of her son. However, she rises above her problems, remains upbeat, and vigorously attacks Henry when he wonders how she can care for a man like Visconti, who has taken all her money.

Visconti is not so well drawn, but his role is minimal. He helps advance the plot. Both Henry and his foil, Wordsworth, are excellently drawn. Wordsworth shows an effective mixture of personal freedom and dependence upon Aunt Augusta. Though he is her happy shepherd boy when Augusta first meets him, when he loses his "bebi gel," Wordsworth's life turns tragic and he is killed in an attempt to get her back from Visconti.

Henry shows greater complexity and an ability to develop that the reader finds convincing. When Henry criticises Visconti's son, Mario, because he doesn't "like a man who cries," the reader recalls that Henry neither laughs nor cries. Yet he is man capable of both by story's end. After his first trip to Brighton with Aunt Augusta, Henry acquires some of her toughness and displays it to the police. Still his cure is not effected. He does backslide. Though he had earlier told the police that marijuana leads no more inevitably to dope addiction than a glass of wine leads to alcoholism, he later scolds the American girl, Tooley, for smoking marijuana.

Even after the long struggle for life he undergoes on his journey across Europe to the East, Henry is not cured. He has indeed grown and misses his travels with his aunt, yet he is still tempted to marry the staid Miss Keane and settle down to a life of her tatting and his growing dahlias. The book's ending might be hyperbolic, in keeping with so boisterous a comedy, but we are convinced Henry has journied a long way. When the CIA man refers to his aunt as a "shady character," Henry's response shows a believable progress: "I would have certainly called her shady myself nine nonths ago, and yet now there seemed nothing so very wrong in her *curriculum vitae*, nothing so wrong as thirty years in a bank." The nine months have passed, and Henry has been very convincingly born again.

## Chapter Fourteen

## *THE HONORARY CONSUL* (1973)

*The Honorary Consul* picks up in the Argentine and Paraguay where *Travels With My Aunt* left us, but it deals with a very different sort of comedy. It is Greene's peculiar version of absurdist comedy, seen already—for example— in *The Comedians* and in *A Burnt-Out Case*. The novel appears an indictment of *machismo*, and yet it is not entirely so since this South American equivalent of Roman *virtus* does have within it the possibilities of heroism and idealism. In fact, one might see here another instance of the excessive or misdirected virtue theme we have seen already and will see again in our next novel.

The story opens in a small town in northern Argentina to which Dr. Plaar has returned from Buenos Aires. He and his mother had once been forced to separate here from his idealistic father, now in prison or dead. Plaar is contacted in this town by schoolboy friends who have turned revolutionary and operate out of Paraguay. They prevail upon him to furnish seemingly harmless information about the American ambassador's itinerary in return for which they will try to effect the release of his father from prison.

Plaar cannot take seriously, or suspect real harm in, these boyhood friends, one of whom—Leon Rivas— is a resigned priest. Nonetheless, when these amateurs mistakenly capture the English Honorary Consul, thinking him the American Ambassador, Plaar is forced to take them seriously. The revolutionaries will not give up the consul, Charley Fortnum, without getting at least half as many released prisoners as an ambassador would bring. They cannot be convinced that this friendly alcoholic is only an honorary consul (honorary they construe as honorable) and will bring nothing. The comedy has become grim.

Plaar, who is having an affair with Fortnum's wife, a former prostitute, does everything to get Fortnum released. His motives are not entirely clear. Certainly he feels some guilt over his part in the kidnap and some fear that the wife and his baby that Clara carries will fall to him should Fortnum die. Yet these reasons will not sufficiently explain his concern. Perhaps he is jealous, as Leon suggests, of Fortnum's ability to love his wife, or love anyone. He is another of Greene's "disengaged" characters, one who grows and comes some way toward bringing together a divided self.

In any event, Plaar's efforts are fruitless since no one is interested in Fortnum and his sinecure. On his return to the prisoner, Plaar is himself held captive to care for Fortnum, who has been wounded in trying to escape. All Plaar's efforts to convince Leon Rivas to let Fortnum go are fruitless. Despite his compassion, Leon is loyal to his absent commander, known in code as El Tigre, and believes a greater cause is being served, even if Fortnum must die.

The hideout is spotted from a helicopter, parachutists are landed, and Fortnum is saved. All others are killed, and the police, without scruple, attribute Plaar's death to the idealistic little priest, Leon Rivas, who in fact died trying to save Plaar from parachutists' bullets.

By this time Fortnum has learned his wife was his friend's mistress and her baby Plaar's son. Though he first experiences difficulty in forgiving her unfaithfulness, he eventually realizes this young girl would not learn faithfulness at her place of employment, "You don't learn love from a customer in a brothel."

Greene's epigraph for the novel is from Thomas Hardy, "All things merge in one another—good into evil, generosity into justice, religion into politics." He might have added, "comedy into tragedy" and vice versa. Greene's later work has reflected more and more a comic view of life, and that view is given expression by the unattractive Dr. Humphries, "Contrary to common belief, the truth is nearly always funny. It's only tragedy which people bother to imagine or invent." The central action of the novel is, of course, comic—the absurd kidnapping of the wrong man. Tragedy enters with *machismo.*

For Leon Rivas *machismo* does not, however, take the common romantic form Plaar finds in a novel by Saavedra: "To fight for one's honor with knives over a woman, that belonged to another, an absurdly outdated world, which had ceased to exist except in the romantic imagination of writers like Saavedra. Honor meant nothing to the starving. To them belonged the more serious fight for survival."

For Leon Rivas, *machismo* resides in the struggle for the survival of the starving, a struggle in the face of whatever overwhelming odds. Leon must force the British to ransom Fortnum with ten of his own people, and failing that Fortnum must be killed lest Leon's men be thought bluffers in the future. His orders had been given by El Tigre. His honor lies in obeying, despite all natural inclination to the contrary. Thus, Plaar and the rebels die. At novel's end, however, we are back in the black comic frame. The heroic Leon is blamed for Plaar's murder; Fortnum, who lacked all *machismo*, gets the girl, and Jorge Julio Saavedra delivers an absurd eulogy that makes Plaar into a *macho hombre*.

Once again, the novel depicts a spoilt priest. Leon Rivas, however, is not at all like those other spoilt priests, Querry or Brown in the two previously considered novels. Plaar perhaps shares Querry's or Brown's symptoms of the fall from grace and vocation. Leon, on the contrary, has really pursued his vocation in the best way he knows. One senses that the Church around him has lost her way. When the Yankees shot a guerrilla priest, Father Rivas had spoken out, "I only said that unlike Sodom the Church did sometimes produce one just man, so perhaps she would not be destroyed like Sodom. The police reported me to the Archbishop and the Archbishop forbade me to preach any more. Oh well, poor man, he was very old and the General liked him, and he thought he was doing right, rendering to Caesar . . ."

The fact that the Church gives priority to one half of Christ's injunction, "Render to Caesar the things that are Caesar's" over the other, "and to God, the things that are God's," has forced Leon to work for the poor in another way. The author has created a character worthy of comparison with his whisky priest in *The Power and the Glory*. He has the humility of that priest—"Oh you must not think we are all of us bad Christians as I am, he says to his captive, Fortnum. And he has the sense of call that the Mexican priest had. He will even kill a man since no one else should bear the burden of his responsibility. Fortnum should make his peace with God, but in the end Leon is ready to do something he detests but believes necessary. He is caught between *machismo* and Christian virtue.

The novel is replete with well-drawn characters. Edwardo Plaar knows "how to fuck [not] how to love." He is happy with a prostitute because one goes to her to get something, not to give something. Yet Plaar's attitudes toward women, as seen also in his attitude to a question from Clara he had not heard— "It could not have been very important. The only questions of importance were those which a man asked himself"—were determined in part by his mother. Her husband's giving his life for his home and ideals is only an inconvenience to her as she grows fat eating eclairs in Buenos Aires. And, indeed, her husband might have been "a man who never knew what love meant," though we have only Señora Plaar's word for that. Was he one who sacrificed Christian love to *machismo?*

While Edwardo Plaar is a cold man who is willing to seduce the wife of a friend, he does involve himself for the sake of his father, and for his friend, Leon. And, however impure his motives for trying to save Fortnum, the efforts, which finally cost his life, seem too complex to be inspired merely by guilt or selfishness. Was his final act one of *machismo* or Christian love or do the two come together here? Even the cuckolded Fortnum can forgive him. When Clara says of Plaar, "I knew then [when he wished Clara to abort her baby] he could never love me," Fortnum responds: "Perhaps he's begun, Clara. Some of us . . . we are a bit slow . . . it's not so easy to love . . . we make a lot of mistakes." He went on for the sake of saying something, "I hated my father . . . I did not much like my [first] wife . . . But they were not really bad people . . . that was only one of my mistakes. Some of us learn to read quicker than others . . . Ted [Plaar ] and I were both bad at the alphabet."

Charley Fortnum also proves a complex character. A self-pitying alcoholic, he is sized up by Plaar at first meeting as one with whom Plaar is not likely to have much in common in the future. The words prove ironic, not merely because they eventually have the same woman in common, but because Charley Fortnum has a quality Plaar does see and does not himself possess, love. He can love and he can forgive a woman.

The characters continually surprise us with a complexity we do not at first notice. In the beginning, Jorge Saavedra seems the epitome of all that Greene dislikes in a writer. Not only are his novels tragic and filled with antiquated *machismo*, but they do not treat of current matters because current matters make a writer topical. We are reminded of Bernard Shaw's stricture, that he who would write for all time, writes for no time. Still Saavedra is no buffoon, and Plaar, who does not enjoy his books, finds a really perceptive quality in the man who reads his motives so precisely. Saavedra seems rather a man of some talent, victimized by the excesses of an ancient tradition.

The lesser characters are also complex. Clara, Marta, Aquino, Perez are none of them fully rounded, but all have in their brief roles the ability to surprise us.

Though the characters are effectively drawn, the novel suffers some from prolixity. Like *A Burnt Out Case,* but not to so great an extent, the fable is not vehicle enough for the talk. This is particularly true of Part Five, one third of the book, where all are in Pablo's house waiting the ransom or death of Fortnum. The topic turns quite naturally to God and to love. There is little action, not even the dialectic that springs from the argument. Leon Rivas has his own quite interesting way of explaining evil. God is evil as well as good. But the latter prevails, and when Leon advances an optimistic belief in the love of God, we are reminded in part of Shaw's Creative Evolution and in part of Chardin's theory of evolution:

> "But I believe in Christ," Father Rivas said, "I
> believe in the Cross and the Redemption. The Redemption
> of God as well as of Man. I believe that the day-side
> of God, in one moment of happy creation, produced
> perfect goodness, as a man might paint one perfect

> picture. God's good intention for once was completely fulfilled so that the night-side can never win more than a little victory here and there. With our help. Because the evolution of God depends on our evolution. Every evil act of ours strengthens His night-side, and every good one helps His day-side. We belong to Him and He belongs to us. But now at least we can be sure where evolution will end one day—it will end in a goodness like Christ's. It is a terrible process all the same and the God I believe in suffers as we suffer while He struggles against Himself—against His evil side."

The thoughts engage us, but Plaar's attempts to taunt Rivas and to engage him in argument become repetitious and do not hold our interest.

There is, however, another insight in this section that is engaging. Leon spends many of his last hours reading a detective story. Such stories offer ritual and order in a world that has renounced the old ritual and order.

> "What are you reading, Leon?" Doctor Plaar asked, "Do you still read your breviary?"
> "I gave that up years ago."
> "What have you got there?"
> "Only a detective story. An English detective story."
> "A good one?"
> "I am no judge of that. The translation is not very good, and with this sort of book I can always guess the end."
> "Then where is the interest?"
> "Oh, there is a sort of comfort in reading a story where one knows what the end will be. The story of a dream world where justice is always done. There were no detective stories in the age of faith—an interesting point when you think of it. God used to be the only detective when people believed in Him. He was law. He was order. He was good. Like your Sherlock Holmes. It was He who purused the wicked man for punishment and discovered all. But now people like the General make law and order."

The fictional detective became the new instrument of goodness and justice when God was asked to resign.

Greene's obsession with Americanism makes its way into this novel also. Pyle's argument for a Third Force reappears, "The General has one great quality [for the Yankees], like Papa Doc used to have in Haiti. He is anti-communist." American involvement is alluded to also in the killing of the Columbian priest, but for the most part this concern of Greene's does not intrude. The occasional references to the Coca Cola sign that "glowed in scarlet letters like the shrine of a saint" is enough to remind us of an American presence in this dictatorship.

A word ought to be said about Greene's style. He seldom says the obvious or uses a cliche. He can be almost cryptic at times, particularly when an action leads up to what could be an obvious conclusion. For example, one chapter concludes with three parachutists approaching Dr. Plaar and Leon Rivas, and the next chapter begins in the cemetery with Señora Plaar dressed in black. The murder has been skipped, and we have avoided the possibility of melodrama. Also, there is just a moment of delay, time enough to raise questions, arouse suspense.

In the book's second chapter, after, the exposition of chapter one, Dr. Plaar's office phone rings, "Never before had they telephoned him so openly." The change is abrupt. Who are "they"? They have played no part in the earlier exposition, which has however set the tone of *machismo* in which we will eventually hear these revolutionaries. Greene is master of this stylistic brevity that hurries us along, providing a minimum of information and a maximum of questions.

The novel is also a fine example of Greene's standard structuring. Part One opens *in medias res*. Part Two flashes back to provide three chapters of necessary background. Then the remaining three parts are in the present, with an occasional reference to the past. The structure is effective, and the prolix fifth part is at least not a flaw in the structure, which probably could not have sustained the philosophizing any earlier.

Ultimately, however, the novel's peculiar strength lies in the balanced and dramatic realization of the struggle between two spirits, *machismo* and Christian virtue. No sides are chosen. Clearly, in the machismo of Saavedra's novels, we are meant to see that South America suffers too much from the influence of "Rousseau and Chateaubriand." Yet Christianity, which stresses rendering to Caesar, might not have conceived of the twentieth-century Caesars Leon Rivas rejects. "Christ had no idea of the kind of world we would be living in now. Render unto Caesar, but when *our* Caesar uses napalm and fragmental bombs . . .The Church lives in time too."

Leon offers us perhaps a better channelled *machismo*, and a responsive Christianity. We emerge from the novel with no greater certainty than he had how to choose between the two. Still, we know that for a moment, when he and Plaar die, we have seen the two spirits blend.

## Chapter Fifteen

# *THE HUMAN FACTOR* (1978)

*The Human Factor* offers the reader themes that have been dominating the author's thoughts ever since his first novel: betrayal, flight, escape that is not true escape because it is solitude, and a self that is divided.

The novel's epigram is from Conrad: "I only know that he who forms a tie is lost. The germ of corruption has entered into his soul." Maurice Castle's soul is corrupted because a tie of gratitude exists between him and a Communist friend.

The novel may, in part, be suggested by Greene's friend and former superior in British Secret Intelligence, Kim Philby. However, Greene had written 25,000 words of the novel before Philby's defection. When Philby wrote his story, *My Secret War*, Greene put the novel aside for ten years.[1] Moreover, we have already noted another reason why we know this story arose independently of Philby's case. Greene anticipated the novel by his 1930 story, "I Spy."

*The Human Factor* is Greene's first espionage novel since *Our Man in Havana* in 1958. Maurice Castle works for the British Secret Service in London and has, we learn halfway through the novel, become a double agent. He has agreed to leak information to the Russians to help thwart "Uncle Remus," a plan devised by England, the United States, and South Africa, to preserve apartheid in South Africa, even to use nuclear weapons for the purpose. Castle has not become a Communist, will not support them in Europe, but owes a Communist friend a favor for helping his black wife, Sarah, escape from South Africa. Also he owes his wife's people something better than apartheid.

The leak in his office is discovered, however, and his more flamboyant companion, Arthur Davis, is suspected and eliminated. Dr. Emmanuel Percival poisons him. Castle now knows he must cease passing information or British Secret Service will discover they have killed the wrong man. He cannot resist one last message, though, when Cornelius Muller, a chief of South African secret police, passes it on to him. Suspecting his cover has been blown, Castle sends his wife and son off to his mother's on the pretext that he and his wife have quarreled. Then he gives an emergency call, and the Russians whisk him out of the country to Moscow. They try to make good their promise to have his wife and child follow, but British Secret Service makes it impossible for Sarah to take the boy when it learns that Sam is not Castle's boy, but the boy of an African who is still alive. The novel ends, then, in bleak fashion when Maurice is permitted to phone from Moscow and learns that his family cannot come. He has escaped into a private prison.

*The Human Factor* makes the reader think Greene is again exemplifying the virtue of disloyalty, for he does everything he can to enlist our sympathy for Castle. He is a more engaging person than are the secret service men he works for; we understand his allegiance to an old friend who saved his wife's life; and we have no sympathy for "Uncle Remus." Nonetheless, Greene is not this time trying to exonerate his character or asking us to agree with Castle, only perhaps asking that we understand and forgive him. What Greene is doing here is what he did in *The Heart of the Matter*, showing how a virtue run wild corrupts. Castle is a victim of gratitude much as Scobie had been a victim of pity.

In chatting with his wife, Sarah, before she learns that he has been spying, Castle remarks:

> "I don't have any trust in Marx or Lenin any more than
> I have in St. Paul, but haven't I the right to be grateful?"
> "Why do you worry so much about it? No one would say
> you were wrong to be grateful, I'm grateful too.
> Gratitude's all right if . . ."
> "If . . .?"
> "I think I was going to say if it doesn't take you too far."

And as Scobie had an excessive pity even as a boy, Maurice Castle had an exaggerated gratitude. He is talking later with his mother:

> "Was I a nervous child?"
> "You always had an exaggerated sense of gratitude for
> the least kindness. It was a sort of insecurity,
> though why you should have felt insecure with me and
> your father . . . You once gave away a good fountain
> pen to someone at school who had offered you a bun
> with a piece of chocolate inside."

Then, at the novel's end, when Castle is isolated in Russia, Sarah asks him in their phone conversation how he is:

> "Oh, everyone is very kind. They have given me a sort
> of job. They are grateful to me. For a lot more than
> I ever intended to do." He said something she didn't

> understand because of a crackle on the line—something about a fountain pen and a bun which had a bar of chocolate in it. "My mother wasn't far wrong."

Though we might make moral judgments about Castle, we certainly also make them about British, South African, and American Intelligence. Percival and Hargreaves dispose of their own man, Davis, on the flimsiest of evidence. He likes the "good life" and that makes him suspect to these two, who discuss him over gourmet luncheons. Daintry, the security officer who checks the leak, comes off much better than his colleagues. However, Daintry's conscience makes him a questioner of his employer's ethics, and a fellow-sufferer with Castle. He is not cut from the same cloth as Percival, Muller, and even the somewhat more human Hargreaves.

Most of the novel's thematic effect is achieved through its structure and shifting point of view. Greene divides his story into six parts, each part having from two to eight chapters, and most of the chapters having still further sub-divisions. The effect he achieves through so many short, tight scenes is to be extremely allusive. The novel is much fuller through its suggestiveness. Typically, too, Greene offers no authorial comment on the action, but his juxtaposed scenes comment on each other. Thus, in successive scenes Percival's lack of ideals is counterpointed by Daintry's soul searching. Right after the funeral for Davis, Sir John Hargreaves and Dr. Emmanuel Percival sit down to their usual elaborate dish and elegant wine:

> Sir John Hargreaves crouched in his chair and buried himself deep in the wine list. He looked unhappy—perhaps only because he couldn't make up his mind between St. Emilion and Medoc. At last he made his decision and his order. "I sometimes wonder why you are with us, Emmanuel."
>
> " You've just said it, I grew up. I don't think Communism will work—in the long run—any better than Christianity has done, and I'm not the Crusader type. Capitalism or Communism? Perhaps God is a Capitalist. I want to be on the side most likely to win during my lifetime. Don't look shocked, John. You think I'm a cynic, but I just don't want to waste a lot of time. The side that wins will be able to build the better hospitals, and give more to cancer research—when all this atomic nonsense is abandoned. In the meanwhile I enjoy the game we're all playing. Enjoy. Only enjoy.

> I don't pretend to be an enthusiast for God or Marx. Beware of people who believe. They aren't reliable players. All the same one grows to like a good player on the other side of the board—it increases the fun."

Ironically Percival, who has murdered for his side, does not believe in that side as much as does Castle who has betrayed it. Percival's attitudes receive the deadliest, though still implicit, condemnation when we read in the next scene of Daintry's return from the funeral. Daintry allows himself to be plied with whisky by an old acquaintance from whom he cannot detach himself, then eats his lunch alone in four minutes while he mulls over Davis' death and wrestles with the temptation to resign:

> His lunch lasted for less than four minutes, but it seemed to him quite a long time because of his thoughts. His thoughts wobbled like a drunken man's. He thought first of Doctor Percival and Sir John Hargreaves going off together down the street in front of him when the service was over, their heads bent like conspirators. He thought next of Davis. It wasn't that he had any personal liking for Davis, but his death worried him. He said aloud to the only witness, which happened to be a sardine tail balanced on his fork, "A jury would never convict on that evidence." Convict? He hadn't any proof that Davis had not died, as the postmortem showed, a natural death—cirrhosis was what one called a natural death. He tried to remember what Doctor Percival had said to him on the night of the shoot. He had drunk too much that night, as he had done this morning, because he was ill at ease with people whom he didn't understand.

Such positioning is typical of the entire book, and much of Greene's writing. A comic scene in which Castle accompanies Daintry to his daughter's wedding is set against the scene in which Davis is found dead; and as Daintry's estranged wife screams at Daintry that he has broken an "irreplaceable" porcelain owl, he is absorbed with the destruction of a more irreplaceable man.

Likewise, in the novel's first part, three scenes at Sir John Hargreaves' offer us Sir John with Daintry, Percival and the other hunters invited out for the day; then Sir John, Daintry, and Percival alone; finally Daintry and Percival. With each scene, the shades of difference in these Intelligence men are seen. And against the progressive insight we are offered of the ruthlessness of Hargreaves and Percival in their attempt to ferret out the traitor, the author has set the previous chapter in which that traitor is glimpsed in a domestic scene with his wife Sarah, his son Sam, who has the measles, and his most unferocious boxer, Buller.

Remarks about scenes that I have removed from context might suggest that Greene is obvious in his manipulation of scenery. He is not. Take, for example, his grand scene, when Cornelius Muller comes to Castle's house. He is an old enemy of the Castles from their days in South Africa, having tried to incarcerate Sarah and prevent Castle from keeping company with this black woman. Now he has been invited to dinner because Castle's job demands it. England must work closely with South Africa and the United States in "Uncle Remus." During the early part of the visit, Sarah remains upstairs to minimize the uneasiness of the reunion with Muller, who knows nothing about Maurice Castle having married her. Nevertheless, everything in Muller's conversation—generalizations about Blacks, questions as to how Castle sneaked his mistress out of South Africa—conspire to embarrass Muller when Sarah will eventually join the men. Yet both Castle and the reader are genuinely surprised when the awaited confrontation occurs, and Muller handles the situation with perfect aplomb.

> Castle called out "Sarah, bring Sam down to say goodnight to Mr. Muller."
> "You are married?" Muller asked.
> "Yes."
> "I'm all the more flattered to be invited to your home. I brought with me a few little presents from South Africa, and perhaps there's something your wife would like. But you haven't answered my question. Now that we are working together—as I wanted to before, you remember—couldn't you tell me how you got that girl out? It can't harm any of your old agents now, and it does have a certain bearing on Uncle Remus, and the problems we have to face together. Your country and mine—and the States, of course—have a common frontier now."
> "Perhaps she'll tell you herself. Let me introduce her and my son, Sam." They came down the stairs together as Cornelius Muller turned.
> "Mr. Muller was asking how I got you into Swaziland, Sarah."
> He had underestimated Muller. The surprise which he had planned failed completely. "I'm so glad to meet you,

> Mrs. Castle," Muller said and took her hand.
> "We just failed to meet seven years ago," Sarah said.
> "Yes. Seven wasted years. You have a very beautiful wife, Castle."

Muller turns out to be more chameleon than bigot.

Effective as Greene's structuring of individual scenes is, his handling of point of view is as impressive. Throughout most of the novel, the focus is on Castle. We see his view of reality. Yet Greene frequently works with a multiple point of view, as did William Faulkner or Greene's long-time favorite, Robert Browning. He differs from these writers insofar as he more often does so in the third person than in the first.

Greene offers us scenes from the point of view of each major character, but perhaps the best example of this shifting focus occurs at the time Castle's treason is about to be discovered. We move from Castle, to Percival, back to Castle, then to Daintry. The technique is most effective. Castle makes his emergency preparation, having sent his wife to his mother's; then we move to Percival and Hargreaves who, because of a tip from Muller, realize Castle, and not Davis whom they have murdered, may be guilty of leaking information; next we return to Castle and to Daintry, sent by Percival to check on Castle, who does not answer his phone; finally we have Daintry giving his report to Percival.

What makes for the effectiveness of the chapter is that we experience the discovery of the real spy, its effect on the main characters, and what it reveals about each of those characters without obvious staging. Pragmatist that he is, Percival is little disturbed that he has destroyed an innocent man in Davis. Hargreaves shows somewhat more sensitivity. However, the chapter develops more fully the complexity of Castle and Daintry. Castle has been forced into the dilemma of needing to terminate his reports to the Communists or be identified as the leak now that Davis is dead and at the same time not wanting Percival and others to think Davis guilty. Thus, over drinks with Daintry, he defends Davis' innocence while trying to show the possibility of several others being the leak.

The next scene belongs to Daintry and is one of the finest in the novel. Having left Castle's house, Daintry drives to a bar, where he tries to call Percival and angrily assert he is all wrong in his suspicions about Castle. The man has merely had an argument with his wife and is staying home drinking, not answering the phone. Percival's phone is busy, and Daintry must wait at the bar. When Daintry finally gets through to Percival, however, his anger takes a different direction. He tells Percival that he has killed the wrong man. Castle is the leak. The reader is stunned, but the scene is effective. In the time between the two calls, Castle's certainty that Davis was innocent works on Daintry and quite understandably convinces him that Castle is certain because Castle is himself the leak. Greene's implicit and unobtrusive treatment of the man's reasoning process is stunning.

*The Human Factor* demonstrates why Greene had to drop the distinction between novel and entertainment. More and more the two genres came together because Greene's interest never confined itself merely to story. Character is his abiding interest, as Denis Donoghue has said.[2] In this novel, we have a host of complex characters who are balanced off against one another. Opposed to the lonely and agonizing Daintry is the gregarious and pragmatic Percival. He poisons Davis, but had come to like the man. Nor will he use the word traitor for Davis since he believes in no abstract virtue of loyalty. Since he does not believe in a right or wrong side, he wants to be on the winning side.

Hargreaves pays lip service to democratic ideals, but he is less honest with himself than is Percival. His real feelings make him more clearly akin to Percival than to Daintry. He protests Davis' murder only as much as his self-image demands, having already played Pilate and washed his hand of the matter so that Percival could act.

Cornelius Muller is another subordinate character who is well-drawn. He has the ability to surprise Castle and the reader because, as we have seen, he cannot be explained away as a bigot. He charms Castle's boy, Sam, as only Davis could and seems completely at ease with former enemies now friends. None of the British Secret Service like him. Yet when he turns Castle in, it is not from old grudges but from suspicion that is more genuine than that which killed Davis.

In Sarah, Greene depicts an interesting and complex woman. Though she and Castle share an intense love, they cannot talk about it with others, and though Sarah defends Castle's act against the charges of his mother, she cannot join him at the expense of leaving her son. We believe her pain as we do his. Castle is a masterpiece of complexity because a reader is never quite certain where indignation at allied insensitivity to African Blacks leaves off and excessive gratitude takes over in his motivation

Greene chose an appropriate epigraph from Conrad for the novel. However, he might have used Maurice Castle's own thoughts in having to deal with Cornelius Muller: "An enemy had to remain a caricature if he was to be kept at a safe distance; an enemy should never come alive." Because Maurice Castle does come alive, *The Human Factor* offers us more than the caricature of a traitor.

This last novel returns us full circle to *The Man Within*. As in his first novel, Greene tells a tale of betrayal. He told us the same tale also in his religious novels when he gave us Scobie and Pinkie and Sarah Miles or in his political novels when he gave us Brown or Fowler. Several of these characters too endured lost childhoods that in turn created divided selves.

Once again the continuity of Greene's themes is borne in upon the reader.

## Chapter Sixteen

# CONCLUSION

This study has focused on Greene's novels. I would be remiss, however, not to make some concluding remarks about his work in general. With the exception of his first published book, *Babbling April* (1925), Greene has not published verse, except in private printings. He has been an active essayist, critic, screenwriter, and reporter. He has written a biography and an autobiography. He is, in brief, a thorough man of letters. However, I will limit my backward glance over Greene's work to his three major genres: drama, short story, and novel, particularly since the first two will help us see his very real strengths as a novelist.

The introduction touched lightly on each of Greene's plays. Drama seems a form in which he grows more interested as he grows less interested in films. Nevertheless, it has not absorbed his interest. Three quite effective plays in the '50s were not followed up until he wrote his least effective play, *Carving a Statue*, in the '60s, and that in turn was not followed for eleven years, when *The Return of A. J. Raffles* appeared.

Perhaps Greene has not written regularly enough to develop the craft of playwrighting as he did the craft of the novel. In 1950 he had found it necessary to write *The Third Man* out fully as a story before turning it to a movie script. By 1952, however, he was constructing *The Living Room*'s script directly, a substantial transition in method in so short a time. Still, Greene has not been an unsuccessful playwright. In his *British Dramatists*, he called the morality plays bones without flesh and regretted that modern plays have too often been flesh without bones.[1] To his credit, Greene's own plays do provide both flesh and bones.

Why then have Greene's plays not caught the public's enthusiasm like his novels have? The answer lies in his not being able to transfer his major strengths from one medium to another. Greene's fictional forte has always been characterization. We remember complex characters like Scobie, Leon Rivas, Sarah Miles, Maurice Castle, the Mexican priest, Thomas Fowler and so on. Their complexity usually comes, however, from their struggle to live in two worlds at once. Scobie wants to be faithful to his wife and to his God yet attend the needs of his lover. Maurice wants to remain loyal to his country and family yet help a

Communist friend. Character not only determines plot but is determined by it. The less discursive form has not yet provided for Greene sufficient time and space to develop complex characters.

*Carving a Statue* barely contains a plot. The sculptor discovers his God the Father is really Lucifer but, after that momentary insight, he turns to Lucifer, since he has wedded himself so irrevocably to his art. *The Living Room* and *The Complaisant Lover* depend upon the marriage triangle. In *The Living Room*, no one can solve Rose's problem, and the suggestion that she pray results in her suicide. In *The Complaisant Lover*, the husband lets the triangle continue and the lover seems undone by such a solution. All three plays prove somewhat weaker than the novels in characterization. And all three lean too heavily, for their effect, upon concluding irony.

*The Potting Shed* depends equally heavily upon concluding irony for its effect. The great rationalist, H. C. Callifer, in the end proves to have been converted by the "miraculous" recovery of his son James, but his wife has kept his loss of the rationalist faith from the world. Uncle William, whose prayers have apparently brought James back, has become a priest, lost his faith for thirty years, and now proves not to believe in the miracle. James, in the end, rescues him from his dark night of the soul and brings him back to life. Once again, the ironic conclusion is asked to provide much of the play's effect. Only in *The Return of A. J. Raffles*, which may be the most contrived of the plays in one sense, is a balance kept so that the play's effect is not so dependent upon its ending.

When we turn to the short story, we recognize Greene has had some major successes and yet has not been as accomplished in the form as in the novel. In his weaker stories, the failure seems sometimes due to a dependence upon concluding irony, as in the plays, and sometimes due simply to too much contrivance. We might at first expect that Greene would be very effective in a form that depends upon plot since he is a master story teller. Yet, as I mentioned in discussing the plays, Greene's real strength is characterization and, for his best efforts here, he needs the more roomy confines of the novel. The short story cannot play to Greene's greatest strength.

Though a relatively effective story, "The Blue Film" might exemplify over-reliance upon concluding irony. At his wife's insistence, a middle-aged man brings her to a thirty-year-old "skin flick." To their astonishment, the man himself is featured making love to a girl. An unmistakeable birthmark identifies him. The wife badgers him the rest of the evening, is told he only made the film to help out the girl, who received £50 she needed badly. Later the wife forces her husband to make love to her for the first time in years, and after it the man feels he has betrayed the only woman he ever loved. The story is partly rescued by its not depending exclusively upon the concluding irony: the man's ambiguous comment on his act of betrayal. The effect depends also, of course, upon his discovering himself on the screen. Moreover, depending on a concluding irony will not hurt the short story as much as it will a play. The story's brief effect can be greatly enhanced by a surprise ending provided such an ending flows naturally from the whole incident. The form does not depend, to any great extent, upon character, even though it has often resulted in memorable characters. A play, on the other hand, has a greater dependence upon character. Its effect comes from what characters directly speak to one another and to the audience.

Although "Awful When You Think Of It" uses a concluding irony, its effect depends mainly upon contrivance throughout. While travelling by train, a man amuses himself by guessing what a child will be like when he is a man and by interpreting what his present grimaces might mean. Such quasipathetic fallacies as "There could be no doubt at all that he was saying, 'A pint of the best bitter'" seemed forced, and a bit trite.

With the humility and honesty that always characterize him, Greene acknowledges in his introduction to *Collected Stories* that he will always "remain in this field [the short story] a novelist who happened to write short stories." He provides his own reason:

> The short story as a form bothered me then and a little bored me. One knew too much about the story before one began writing—and then there were all the days of work unrelieved by any surprise. In the far longer work of the novel there were periods of great weariness, but at any moment the unexpected might happen—a minor character would suddenly take control and dictate his words and actions. Somewhere near the beginning, for no reason I knew, I would insert an incident which seemed entirely irrelevant, and sixty thousand words later, with a sense of excitement, I would realize why it was there—the narrative had been working all the time outside my conscious control. But in the short story I knew everything before I began to write—or so I thought.

In discussing Greene's fictional method in the first chapter, we saw that he liked to forget people and incidents and have them emerge from the subconscious as characters and fictional situations. Such a procedure simply is not possible in a form whose effect depends not upon characters but upon plot.

We ought not, however, to dwell too much upon Greene's weaknesses in the short story form. He has written some excellent short stories. Like Keats and unlike—say—Byron, Greene has always been a good critic of his own work. He remarks that, despite his greater success with the novel, he has never written anything better than his four stories: "The Destructors," "A Chance for Mr. Lever," "Under the Garden," and "Cheap in August," and he commends his early "I Spy" for a simplicity of language that his novels of the same period lack. Among the thirty-eight stories in his *Collected Stories*, the ones he names are probably the best, but there are several other well-wrought stories that will help guarantee his reputation as a short story writer, e.g. "Two Gentle People," "A Visit to Morin," "A Discovery in the Woods," "Special Duties," "The Basement Room" (from which a very successful film, *The Fallen Idol*, was made), "Hint of An Explanation," "A Drive in the Country," and "The End of the Party."

The novel finally is the form upon which Greene's reputation will rest. His strengths in the form are many. His themes have remained with him throughout a lifetime. Thus, they are not formulated to help a specific plot along but are part of his vision and have worked their way into many and different plots. "If there are recurrent themes in my novels, it is perhaps only because there have been recurrent themes in my life," Greene tells us in *A Sort of Life*. This ability to work recurrent themes into so many situations is a testimony to their deep-rootedness that we saw earlier is the hallmark of the poet as distinct from the journeyman in fiction.

Another strength of Greene's novels is the strong tension that springs from his playing devil's advocate, the dynamics that occur when his character finds himself divided between loyalties. In his first novel, *The Man Within*, this division was handled crudely, even externalized in the boy's attraction for two different women. In the later novels the struggle is internalized.

It is this enduring ability to internalize struggle that makes character depiction one of Greene's strengths. Sarah Miles is torn between her loyalty to God and her loyalty to her lover. Fowler cannot decide whether he wants to eliminate Pyle for the good of Vietnam or to get his woman back from a rival. The characters are shaded in, rendered complex by internal division. We believe in them because they are not the stuff of which melodrama is made.

One cannot discuss the strengths of Greene's fiction without a word about his style. He learned economy and precision while subeditor for the *Times*. More than for anything else, Greene has struggled for precision, "truth" as he calls it, in form as well as in substance. Following his apprenticeship at the *Times*, the failure of his second and third novels proved a disguised blessing. Not only did he now learn to build upon autobiography, authentic experience, he learned that "action can only be expressed by a subject, a verb, an object, perhaps rhythm—little else. Even an adjective slows the pace or tranquillizes the nerve." And similes, he learned, reflect states of mind, not action.

In the process of his movie reviewing Greene seems to have acquired a feel for cinematic technique, which he applied to his fiction. Certainly, the technique is there. No living novelist has had his work more often transferred to film. Each of these experiences—his sub-editorship, his early fictional failures, his film reviewing—coupled with what Percy Lubbock and Henry James taught him about limiting the center of vision, helped produce the crisp, vivid, fast-moving and clearly focussed style that marks Greene's fiction.

One final element of his style demands mention. Critics have noted his appeal to contemporary taste with a liberal amount of sex. What they have not noted often enough is his restraint in this area. Greene sees a difficulty for the modern novelist in evoking the sex act since it can become too large and unbalance a scene or even a whole book. Thus, he has confessed to disliking Genet, but not to disliking pornography. "Fanny Hill is elegant, well-mannered and is about the baroque quality of the sexual imagination."[1] Sex in his own novels is honest, forthright, but not very detailed. To V. S. Pritchett he acknowledged having none of D. H. Lawrence's ability to deal directly with the intimacies of lovers. Rather, he was able to deal with their habits, quarrels, and petty jealousies.

Since he is a remarkable self critic, Greene has overcome most of his early fictional weaknesses. He corrected the early tendency to distrust autobiographical material because it was supposed to be the mark of a young novelist. Another problem he seems to have corrected is a certain weakness in creating women. Surely he has grown in this regard. In his first twenty-four years as a novelist, he depicted perhaps only two or three complex women: Kate Farrant of *England Made Me* and Sarah Miles of *The End of the Affair*, and possibly Ida Arnold of *Brighton Rock*. In 1953, however, he salvaged the difficult Aunt Helen of *The Living Room*, a woman made for melodrama with her pre-Vatican II theology, and turned her into something more than a stereotyped mother superior. Aunt Helen's fear of death, her closing of the rooms in which someone died, helped explain her hardness. It was a small but significant instance of turning a stock character into something more. Six years later, in what may be his best play—*The Complaisant Lover*—Mary Rhodes emerges as a complex woman (at least for a Greene play) who loves her dull but solid husband, yet will not renounce her more romantic lover. Of course, Greene's great woman character was to come ten years later in *Travels With My Aunt*. Aunt Augusta ranks with Sarah Miles as the best of

Greene's female creations. His next novel, *The Honorary Consul*, had no major women characters, but *The Human Factor* did, and Sarah Castle is much more alive and believable than Greene's early women. He has, then, clearly grown in his ability to create well-rounded women characters.

If there is one weakness that mars some of Greene's more recent novels, it is making his characters too prolix. His favorite novel at the moment seems to be *The Honorary Consul*, and yet this otherwise strong novel is hurt by using characters too evidently as mouthpieces for ideas. Certainly Greene still allows the dynamics of debate, but the characters nevertheless cease on occasion to speak like real characters and serve as puppets for the ventriloquist controlling the debate.

What, finally, Greene's reputation will be a century hence is difficult to predict. He will not be among the number of writers we remember for their style but not for their view of life. Nor will he be among those we remember for substance but not for form, even though he was often enthusiastically embraced for his religious subjects by readers in the '40s and '50s, who forgot him when he ceased writing on those subjects. Some readers have even detected in him a drift from Catholicism, but such a conclusion is founded upon reading his novels as reflections of his own life. We saw earlier that even Evelyn Waugh identified Querry of *A Burnt-Out Case* with the author and determined he was a lost leader. Greene corrected him and wondered what people would think if they saw him at Mass.

The fact is that, while Greene remains a Catholic, religious problems no longer occupy his mind as they did in the '50s. Thus, he has given us few primarily religious novels since that time. "With the approach of death I care less and less about religious truth. One hasn't long to wait for revelation or darkness" (1971). As recently as last year he called himself a "Catholic atheist," but that because he has always had trouble with the concept of God, preferring Chardin's "Noosphere" to the term God, with its anthropomorphic suggestions.

When readers look at Greene a century hence, they will find him more than a religious writer, more—certainly—than a Catholic writer. They will find that for several years he turned to religion as a vehicle to carry his dominant themes and then turned back to other vehicles for the same themes. They will find he also used thematic vehicles for all the pressing issues of an era: the Vietnam War, Papa Doc's tyrannizing over Haiti, the world struggle between Communism and Capitalism (though always fleshed out in specifics), apartheid, Latin-America's struggle for the poor and her efforts both for the freedom of the Church and against the oppressiveness of the Church, as well as of the State. Will these issues seem too topical for posterity or will they prove again that only by localizing one's story in the specifics of a time and place can one appeal to readers of another time and place? He who would write for all time will discover that he writes for no time. Greene may well prove to have written for all time.

## Notes

Chapter 1 1. *New York Times*, 26 February 1978, sect. 6, p. 36.

2. J. S. Ryan, ed., *Gleanings from Greeneland* (Armidale, N.S.W.: University of New England Press), p. 58.

3. Phillips, *Graham Greene*, pp. 133-134.

4. John Atkins, *Graham Greene* (London: Calder and Byars, 1966), p. 86.

5. *New York Times*, 26 February 1978, sect. 6, p. 34.

Chapter 2 1. Graham Greene, *The Man Within* (London: William Heinemann and the Bodley Head, 1929, 1976). This is the Collected Edition, which I use for all the novels in this study, except for those novels that have not yet had such an edition prepared. There are three instances. I use the Bodley Head edition for *Travels With My Aunt* and *The Honorary Consul*, and the Simon and Schuster edition of *The Human Factor*.

2. Philip Stratford, ed., *The Portable Graham Greene* (New York: Viking, 1973), p. 609.

3. Kenneth Allott and Miriam Farris, *The Art of Graham Greene* (London: Hamish Hamilton, 1951), p. 14.

4. Bruno Bettelheim, *The Uses of Enchantment* (New York: Albert A. Knopf, 1976), pp. 159-160.

Chapter 3 1. *New York Times*, 26 February 1978, sect. 6, p. 33.

Chapter 4 1. Herbert Haber, "The Two Worlds of Graham Greene," *Modern Fiction Studies* 3 (Autumn 1957): 256-268. R. W. B. Lewis, "The Trilogy of Graham Greene," *Modern Fiction Studies* 3 (Autumn 1957): 195-215 implicitly agrees with Haber's interpretation.

Chapter 5 1. Phillips, *Graham Greene*, pp. 106-113. For much of my discussion of Greene's films, I am indebted to this work.

Chapter 6 1. Phillips, *Graham Greene*, p. 29.

Chapter 7 1. Phillips, *Graham Greene*, pp. 120-122.

2. Allott and Farris, *The Art of Graham Greene*, pp. 215 ff.

Chapter 8 1. For a full discussion of changes in *The End of the Affair* and how they reflect or betray an author's intentions, v. David Leon Higdon, "'Betrayed Intentions': Graham Greene's *The End of the Affair,"The Library* (March 1979), 70-77.

Chapter 9 1. Philip Rahv, "Wicked American Innocence," review of *The Quiet American*, 21 *Commentary* (May 1956): 488-490.
2. *New York Times*, 11 March 1956, sect. 7, p 1.
3. *New York Times*, 26 August 1956, sect. 7, p. 8.

Chapter 11 1. Dominick P. Consolo, "Graham Greene: Style and Stylistics in Five Novels," in *Graham Greene: Some Critical Considerations*, ed. Robert O. Evans (Lexington: Univ. of Kentuky Press, 1967) pp. 64-65.

Chapter 12 1. Stanley Kauffmann, review of film, "The Comedians," *New Republic*, 2 December 1967.
2. Moira Walsh, review of film, "The Comedians" *America*, 2 December 1967.

Chapter 13 1. Moira Walsh, review of film, "Travels With My Aunt," *America*, 23 December 1972.

Chapter 15 1. *New York Times*, 26 February 1978, sect. 6, p. 46.
2. *New York Times, 26 February 1978, sect. 7, p. 1.*

Chapter 16 1. *New York Times*, 26 February 1978, sect. 6, p. 44.

## BIBLIOGRAPHY

1. Works by Graham Greene

Novels


*The Man Within*. London: Heineman, 1929.
*The Name of Action*. London: Heinemann, 1930 (later withdrawn).
*Rumour at Nightfall*. London: Heinemann, 1939 (later withdrawn).
*Stamboul Train*. London: Heinemann, 1932. Published as *Orient Express*. Garden City: Doubleday, 1932.
*It's A Battlefield*. London: Heinemann, 1934.
*England Made Me*. London: Heinemann, 1935. Reissued as *The Shipwrecked*. New York: Viking Press, 1953.
*A Gun for Sale*. London: Heinemann, 1936. Published as *This Gun for Hire*. Garden City: Doubleday, 1936.
*Brighton Rock*. London: Heinemann, 1938.
*The Confidential Agent*. London: Heinemann, 1939.
*The Power and the Glory*. London: Heinemann, 1940.
*The Ministry of Fear*. London: Heinemann, 1943.
*The Heart of the Matter*. London: Heinemann, 1948.
*The Third Man*. London: Heinemann, 1950.
*The End of the Affair*. London: Heinemann, 1951.
*Loser Takes All*. London: Heinemann, 1955.
*The Quiet American*. London: Heinemann, 1955.
*Our Man in Havana*. London: Heinemann, 1958.
*A Burnt-Out Case*. Stockholm: Norstedt 1960; London: Heinemann, 1961.
*The Comedians*. London: Bodley Head, 1966.
*Travels With My Aunt*. London: Bodley Head, 1969.
*The Honorary Consul*. London: Bodley Head, 1973.
*The Human Factor*. London: Bodley Head, 1978.


Short Stories


*The Basement Room and Other Stories*. London: Cresset, 1935.
*Nineteen Stories*. London: Heinemann, 1947.

*Twenty-One Stories*. London: Heinemann, 1954. Two stories from previous collection dropped and four added.
*A Sense of Reality*. London: Bodley Head, 1963.
*May We Borrow Your Husband*. London: Bodley Head, 1967.
*Collected Stories*. London: Bodley Head and Heinemann, 1973.

Plays

*The Living Room*. Stockholm: Norstedt, 1952. London: Heinemann, 1953.
*The Potting Shed*. New York: Viking, 1957.
*The Complaisant Lover*. London: Heinemann, 1959.
*Carving A Statue*. London: Bodley Head, 1964.
*The Return of A. J. Raffles*. London: Bodley Head, 1975.

Poems

*Babbling April*. Oxford: Blackwell, 1925.
*After Two Years*. Privately Printed, 1949.
*For Christmas*. Privately Printed, 1959.

Travel Books

*Journey Without Maps*. London: Heinemann, 1936.
*The Lawless Roads* London: Longmans Green, 1939.
*In Search of A Character*. London: Bodley Head, 1961.

Essays and Criticism

*British Dramatists*. London: William Collins, 1942.
*Graham Greene on Film: Collected Film Criticism, 1935-1940*. Edited by John Russell Taylor. New York: Simon and Schuster, 1972.
*The Lost Childhood and Other Essays*. London: Eyre and Spottiswoode, 1951.
*Essais Catholiques*. Paris: Editions de Sevill, 1953.
*Collected Essays*. London: Bodley Head, 1969.

Biography and Autobiography

*A Sort of Life*. London: Bodley Head, 1979.
*Lord Rochester's Monkey*. London: Bodley Head, 1974.

Children's Books

*The Little Train*. London: Eyre and Spottiswoode, 1946.
*The Little Fire Engine*. London: Max Parrish, 1950.
*The Little Horse Bus*. London: Max Parrish, 1952.
*The Little Steamroller*. London: Max Parrish, 1953.

2. Works About Graham Greene

Allott, Kenneth and Farris, Mariam. *The Art of Graham Greene*. London: Hamish Hamilton, 1951.

Atkins, John. *Graham Greene*. London: Calder and Byars, 1966.

Boardman, *Graham Greene: The Aesthetics of Exploration*. Gainesville: University of Florida Press, 1971.

Connolly, Francis X. "Inside Modern Man: The Spiritual Adventures of Graham Greene." *Renascence* 1 (1949): 16-24.

De Vitis, A. A. *Graham Greene*. New York: Twayne Publishers, 1964.

Emerson, Gloria. "Our Man in Antibes: Graham Greene." *Rolling Stone*, 9 March 1978, pp. 45-49.

Evans, Robert O., ed. *Graham Greene: Some Critical Considerations*. Lexington: University of Kentucky Press, 1967.

Higdon, David Leon. "'Betrayed Intentions': Graham Greene's *The End of the Affair*. *The Library* 1 (1979): 70-77.

Hynes, Samuel L., ed. *Graham Greene: A Collection of Critical Essays*. Englewood Cliffs, N.J.: Prentice-Hall, 1973.

Kunkel, Francis L. *The Labyrinthine Ways of Graham Greene*. Mamaroneck, N.Y.: Paul P. Appel, 1973.

Lewis, R.W.B. "Graham Greene: The Religious Affair," in *The Picaresque Saint: Representative Figures in Contemporary Fiction*, pp. 220-74, New York: Lippincott, 1959.

*Modern Fiction Studies* 3 (Autumn 1957). Special Graham Greene Number.

O'Faolain, Sean. "Graham Greene, or 'I suffer, therefore I am.'" in *The Vanishing Hero: Studies in Novelists of the Twenties*, pp. 71-97. London: Eyre and Spottiswoode, 1956.

Phillips, Gene D., S. J. *Graham Greene: The Films of His Fiction*. New York: Teachers College Press, 1974.

Pritchett, V.S., "The Human Factor in Graham Greene." *New York Times Magazine*, 26 February 1978, pp. 33-46.

Pryce-Jones, David. *Graham Greene*. New York: Barnes and Noble, 1967.

Ryan, J.S., ed. *Gleanings from Greeneland*. Armidale, N.S.W.: University of New England Press, 1972.

*Renascence* 12 (Fall 1959). Special Graham Greene Number.

*Renascence* 23 (Autumn 1970). Special Graham Greene Number.

Stratford, Philip. *Faith and Fiction: Creative Process in Greene and Mauriac*. Notre Dame: University of Notre Dame Press, 1964.

——, ed. *The Portable Graham Greene*. New York: Viking, 1973.

Sternlicht, Sandford. "Prologue to the Sad Comedies: Graham Greene's Major Early Novels." *Midwest Quarterly* 12 (1971): 427-35.

——. "The Sad Comedies: Graham Greene's Later Novels." *Florida Quarterly* 1 (1968): 65-77.

Traversi, Derek. "Graham Greene: The Earlier Novels." *Twentieth Century* 149 (March 1951): 231-40.

——. "Graham Greene: The Later Novels." *Twentieth Century* 149 (April 1951): 318-28.

Turnell, Martin. *Graham Greene*. Grand Rapids, Mi.: William B. Eerdmans, 1967.

Wolfe, Peter. *Graham Greene the Entertainer*. Carbondale: Southern Illinois University Press, 1972.

Wyndham, Francis. *Graham Greene*. London: Longmans, Green, 1968.

Zabel, Morton D. "Graham Greene: The Best and the Worst," in *Craft and Character in Modern Fiction*, pp. 276-96: New York: Viking, 1957.

**J. G. RIEWALD and J. BAKKER**: *The Critical Reception of American Literature in the Netherlands, 1824-1900:* A Documentary Conspectus from Contemporary Periodicals. Amsterdam 1982. 355 p. Hfl. 70,–

The purpose of this book is to explore the contemporaneous recognition of American literature in nineteenth-century Dutch periodicals and to assess its quality. In order to present a realistic picture of the Dutch response, the study has aimed at complete coverage. Breaking the established pattern in more ways than one, it inaugurates an altogether new type of reception study. It makes available for the first time an organized collection of over three hundred and fifty contemporary reviews, review articles, essays, and notices of thirtyseven American authors from thirty-six nineteenth-century Dutch periodicals. What distinguishes the book from comparable works about the reception of American literature in non-anglophone countries is the systematic presentation and analysis of a hitherto unexplored wealth of data through detailed synopses and quotations, all translated into English. It is, therefore, not only a study of the reception of American literature in nine teenth-century Dutch periodicals, but also a critical survey anthology and bibliography. The book is divided into three Parts, preceded by a Preface and an Introduction. The Introduction includes a comparative analysis of the differences between contemporary American criticism and the contemporary Dutch response, throwing light on the nature and significance of the Dutch recognition. Part I contains the summaries of the reviews and articles devoted to individual authors; in most cases these summaries are preceded by a checklist of Dutch translations of the works written by the author under discussion. These lists – the first of their kind – are reasonably complete. Part II contains the summaries of general and miscellaneous articles on American literature. Part III consists of Notes and the following Appendixes; Appendix 1; Reviewers and Essayists; Biographical Notes; Appendix 2; Initials and Pseudonyms of Unidentified Critics; Appendix 3; An Annotated List of Select Periodicals.

**COLIN PARTRIDGE**: *The Making of New Cultures:* A Literary Perspective. Amsterdam 1982. 131 p. Hfl. 30,–

Over the past five hundred years, countries as different as Brazil, the United States, Australia, Canada, Trinidad and Guatemala have developed distinctive cultures. Because major writers from these regions have made radical analyses of their cultures' formation and growth, the new literatures of these areas offer insights into the processes of cultural development. Writers from new-world societies have examined formative influences, dramatized changes in psycho-social and socio-political relationships, and offered alternative values to those they have seen prevailing in their contemporary societies. Because new-world cultures are less fixed than older cultures in mannered traditions and intellectual styles, the imaginative presentations of committed writers have often been made with a large measure of social idealism. 'The Making of New Cultures' surveys major twentieth-century works from regions as diverse as Brazil, the United States, Australia, Canada, Trinidad and Guatemala. It uses a comparative method to establish categories of concern which reveal the deep cultural preoccupations of writers such as Graciliano Ramos, John Steinbeck, Patrick White, Margaret Laurence, V.S. Naipaul and Miguel Angel Asturias.

## *COSTERUS NEW SERIES*

Volume 1.
Edited by James L. W. West III. Amsterdam 1974. 194 p. Hfl. 40,–

Volume 2.
THACKERAY. Edited by Peter L. Shillingsburg. Amsterdam 1974. 359 p. Hfl. 70,–

Volume 3.
Edited by James L. W. West III. Amsterdam 1975. 184 p. Hfl. 40,–

Volume 4.
Edited by James L.W. West III. Amsterdam 1975. 179 p. Hfl. 40,–

Volume 5-6.
GYASCUTUS. Studies in Antebellum Southern Humorous and Sporting Writing. Edited by James L. W. West III. Amsterdam 1978. 234 p. Hfl. 35,–

Volume 7.
SANFORD PINSKER: The Language of Joseph Conrad. Amsterdam 1978. 87 p. Sold out

Volume 8.
GARLAND CANNON: An Integrated Transformational Grammar of the English Language. Amsterdam 1978. 315 p. Hfl. 60,–

Volume 9.
GERALD LEVIN: Richardson the Novelist: The Psychological Patterns. Amsterdam 1978. 177 p. Hfl. 30,–

Volume 10.
WILLIAM F. HUTMACHER: Wynkyn de Worde and Chaucer's Canterbury Tales. A Transcription and Collation of the 1498 Edition with Caxton² from the General Prologue Through the Knights Tale. Amsterdam 1978. 224 p. Hfl. 40,–

Volume 11.
WILLIAM R. KLINK: S. N. Behrman: The Major Plays. Amsterdam 1978. 272 p. Hfl. 45,–

Volume 12.
VALERIE BONITA GRAY: 'Invisible Man's' Literary Heritage: 'Benito Cereno' and 'Moby Dick'. Amsterdam 1978. 145 p. Hfl. 30,–

Volume 13.
VINCENT DIMARCO and LESLIE PERELMAN: The Middle English Letter of Alexander to Aristotle. Amsterdam 1978. 194 p. Hfl. 40,–

Volume 14.
JOHN W. CRAWFORD: Discourse: Essays on English and American Literature. Amsterdam 1978. 200 p. Hfl. 40,–

Volume 15.
ROBERT F. WILLSON, JR.: Landmarks of Shakespeare Criticism. Amsterdam 1978. 113 p. Hfl. 25,–

Volume 16.
A.H. QURESHI: Edinburgh Review and Poetic Truth. Amsterdam 1978. 61 p. Hfl. 15,–

Volume 17.
RAYMOND J.S. GRANT: Cambridge Corpus Christi College 41: The Loricas and the Missal. Amsterdam 1978. 127 p. Hfl. 30,–

Volume 18.
CARLEE LIPPMAN: Lyrical Positivism. Amsterdam 1978. 195 p. Hfl. 40,–

Volume 19.
EVELYN A. HOVANEC: Henry James and Germany. Amsterdam 1978. 149 p. Hfl. 30,–

Volume 20.
SANDY COHEN: Norman Mailer's Novels. Amsterdam 1979. 133 p. Hfl. 25,–

Volume 21.
HANS BERTENS: The Fiction of Paul Bowles. The soul is the weariest part of the body. Amsterdam 1979. 260 p. Hfl. 50,–

Volume 22.
RICHARD MANLEY BLAU: The Body Impolitic. A reading of four novels by Herman Melville. Amsterdam 1979. 214 p. Hfl. 45,–

Volume 23.
FROM CAXTON TO BECKETT. Essays presented by W.H. Toppen on the occasion of his seventieth birthday, Edited by Jacques B.H. Alblas and Richard Todd. With a foreword by A.J. Fry. Amsterdam 1979. 133 p. Hfl. 30,–

Volume 24.
CAROL JOHNSON: The Disappearance of Literature. Amsterdam 1980. 123 p. Hfl. 25,–

Volume 25.
LINGUISTIC STUDIES offered to Berthe Siertsema, edited by D.J. van Alkemade, A. Feitsma, W.J. Meys, P. van Reenen en J.J. Spa. Amsterdam 1980. 382 p. Hfl. 56,–

Volume 26.
FROM COOPER TO PHILIP ROTH, Essays on American Literature, Presented to J.G. Riewald, on the occasion of his seventieth birthday. Edited by J. Bakker and D.R.M. Wilkinson, with a foreword by J. Gerritsen. Amsterdam 1980. 118 p. Hfl. 25,–

Volume 27.
ALLAN GARDNER SMITH: The Analysis of Motives: Early American Psychology and Fiction. Amsterdam 1980. V,201 p. Hfl. 40,–

Volume 28.
PATRICK D. MORROW: Tradition, Undercut, and Discovery: Eight Essays on British Literature. Amsterdam 1980. 253 p. Hfl. 50,–

Volume 29.
THE ROMANTIC AGE IN PROSE. An Anthology, edited by Alan W. Bellringer and . B. Jones. Amsterdam 1980. 165 p. Hfl. 30,–

Volume 30.
P.J. DE VOOGD: Henry Fielding and William Hogarth. The Correspondences of the Arts. Amsterdam 1981. 195 p. Hfl. 40,–

Volume 31.
GERALD M. BERKOWITZ: Sir John Vanbrugh and the End of Restoration Comedy. Amsterdam 1981. 232 p. Hfl. 50,–

Volume 32.
C.C. BARFOOT: The thread of connection. Aspects of Fate in the Novels of Jane Austen and Others. Amsterdam 1982. 225 p. Hfl. 45,–

Volume 33.
J.G. RIEWALD AND J. BAKKER: The Critical Reception of American Literature in the Netherlands, 1824-1900. A Documentary Conspectus from Contemporary Periodicals. Amsterdam 1982. 355 p. Hfl. 70,–

Volume 34.
COLIN PARTRIDGE: The Making of New Cultures: A Literary Perspective. Amsterdam 1982. 131 p. Hfl. 30,–

Volume 35.
RICHARD S. MOORE: That Cunning Alphabet. Melville's Aesthetics of Nature. Amsterdam 1982. 224 p. Hfl. 40,–

Volume 36.
JOHN FLETCHER: A Wife for a Moneth. Edited by David Rush Miller. Amsterdam 1983. 286 p. Hfl. 60,–

Volume 37.
J. BAKKER: Fiction as Survival Strategy. A Comparative study of the Major works of Ernest Hemingway and Saul Bellow. Amsterdam 1983. 220 p.Hfl. 45,–

Volume 38.
HENRY J. DONAGHY: Graham Greene: An Introduction to His Writings. Amsterdam 1983. 124 p. Hfl. 25,–

USA/Canada: Humanities Press Inc., 171 First Avenue, Atlantic Highlands, N.J. 07716/USA

Japan: United Publishers Services Ltd., Kenkyu-sha Building, 9, Kanda Surugadai, 2-chome, Chiyoda-ku, Tokyo, Japan

And others: Editions Rodopi B.V., Keizersgracht 302-304, 1016 EX Amsterdam, Telephone (020) – 22 75 07